C000226168

About the Author

Robert Llewellyn was born in 1956 in Northampton. He was first confronted with the women's movement when he attended school in Oxfordshire with a proto feminist who called him 'a sexist git'.It took him many years to recover from this early onslaught to his developing masculine persona, but he went on to learn and grow.

By 1975 he was living in a feminist commune near Regent's Park where he learned not to use 'the C word' and do a great deal of washing up. By the late seventies he had been in a men's group which met over a book shop in Hackney on rainy Tuesday evenings.

In the early 80s he co-founded the ultra right-on theatrical men's group, 'The Joeys' and since then has written extensively about and been deeply involved in all issues concerned with the male position in an emerging hypothetical post-patriarchal society. It is only now, 20 years later, that he is able to look back over this period and start drawing conclusions.

Robert lives in London, Los Angeles, Australia and Gloucestershire. He is involved in a deeply complex, difficult, passionate, long term, committed relationship and is not, at present, available for any low impact sexual dalliance.

THE RECONSTRUCTED HEART

THE RECONSTRUCTED HEART

How to spot the Difference between a Normal Man and one who does the Housework, is Great in Bed, and doesn't get all iffy when you mention Words like Love and Committment

ROBERT LLEWELLYN

SIMON & SCHUSTER

LONDON·SYDNEY·NEW YORK·TOKYO·SINGAPORE·TORONTO

First published in Great Britain by
Simon & Schuster Ltd in 1992
A Paramount Communications Company

Simon & Schuster Ltd
West garden Place
Kendal Street
London W2 2AQ

Simon & Schuster of Australia Pty Ltd
Sydney

A CIP catalogue record for this book is
available from the British Library
ISBN 0-671-71182-2

Photoset in Garamond with Bodoni by
Derek Doyle & Associates, Mold, Clwyd
Printed and bound in Great Britain by
HarperColins Manufacturing, Glasgow

The author would like to thank the following people for their kind and patient understanding as he struggled with his subject. Without their support, criticism and ability to listen to his drivel, this book would not have been possible.

Judy Pascoe, Jenny Landreth, Jack Klaff, Brenda and Reg Allen, Dewi Matthews, Christophe Egret, Gill Girling, Loretta Sacco, Sonia Serafin, Martin Pople, Debora John Wilson, Gill Anderson, Chris Eymard, Bernie Evans, Nigel Ordish, Graham Allum, Nigel Planer, John McKay, Stephen Garrett, Tony Garnett, Susie Dee, Madge Fletcher, Mary Pachnos and Carol O'Brien.

in memory of
Michael Baumgarten

Contents

Introduction

There are two types of people. Men and women. It has always been, as long as we've been recording history, the men who rule, the women who do the washing up. The argument only started when some women said, 'We want to rule, you do the washing up.' The argument got more complicated when some men said, 'Okay, we'll do some of the washing up, and you can do some of the ruling.' Now things are getting indescribably more complicated because some men, only one or two now, but a growing number are saying, 'I'll do all the washing up, you go and rule, and keep out of my kitchen.'

This book is not a personal manifesto, although it does come out of a lifelong obsession with these arguments. It focuses on the male response to feminism from 1970 to 1990. It looks at the men who want to do all the washing up, and the men who don't do any and compares the two. It compares their habits, attitudes, behavioural patterns and sexuality. It gives hints and tips for any woman who is interested in finding a reconstructed male partner, starting some sort of relationship with him and getting involved in the strains, changes and difficulties this will entail.

During the research period for this book I used all the very latest techniques in data collection, many along similar lines as those used by opinion pollsters in the run up to the '92 UK general election. I also formed a loose-knit and informal study group, a cross-section of men who I interviewed over a ten-year period. Allied to this were numerous visits to weekend intensive seminars, group therapy sessions in prisons and men's houses, initiation ceremonies on college campuses, in sweat lodges, nude psycho-drama drumming marathons and genital balancing weekends. A full list of research notes can be found at the end of the book, just past the section on sex.

Generally speaking the work has involved interviewing and talking to men; after all, that is the subject matter of the work. However at one point I did interview a few women and come across this rather startling example of the breakdown in communication between the sexes. It was this one piece of information which inspired the whole book.

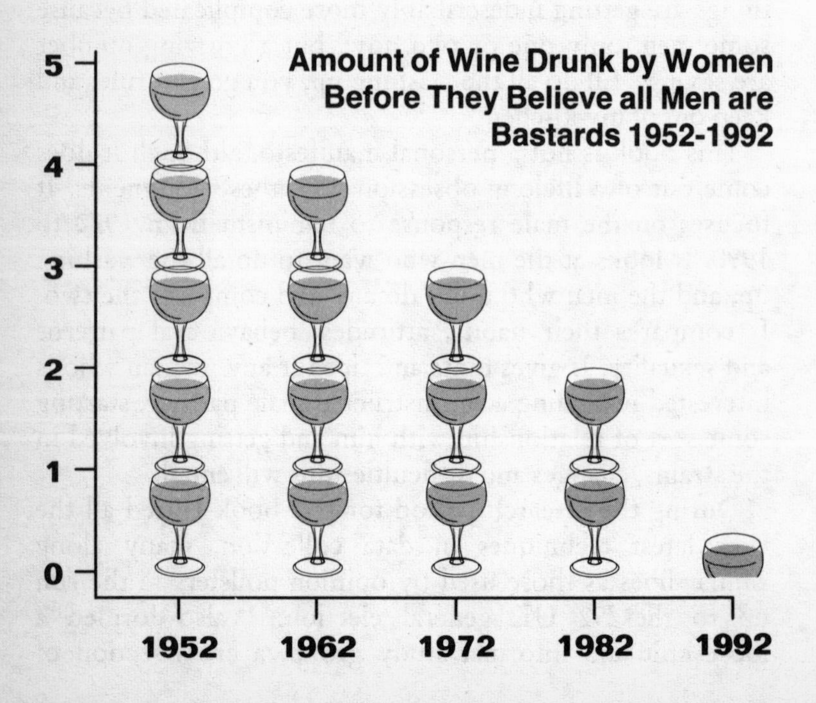

As we can see from this graph, the amount of wine a woman has to drink before she believes all men are bastards has fallen consistently over the past twenty years. I have asked many specialists in the field if they can find any reason for this, but no one seems to have an answer. As one Professor Emeritus told me, 'It's just one of those things ladies tend to think.'

chapter 1

History*

As any historian will tell you, events don't happen, they evolve. Inventions, such as motor vehicles, don't suddenly drive out of sheds and change the world. There are always dozens of examples of really embarrassing cars which are pushed out of sheds for years and thankfully ignored. The designers stand by them proudly until they notice that the contraption makes people wince and look away. The machine is then pushed back in again and the process starts afresh.

It's exactly the same with the case of the apparently sudden appearance of the 'new' or reconstructed man. He did not suddenly pop up out of the blue, naked, in front of a feminist woman, washed, sexually ready and say, '*Hi, my name's Roger, if you're interested in making love I'm here, if not, fine, but it would be great to talk sometime, about love, sex and the difficulties you've had with other men in the past.*'

The reconstructed heart, like all socio-political phe-

* Well, let's start as we mean to go on. The word history is very contentious, some people believing it is the patriarchal recording of events, i.e. his story. In fact the word was first recorded by Caxton, and comes from the Latin *historia*- Gr *historia*, learning or knowing by inquiry, plus the old French *histor* meaning learned wise man. There you go, see. *Patriarchy*, chapter one, page one. You can't get away from it.

nomena, evolved slowly and out of thousands of chaotic and, at first glance, unconnected events, ideas and activities. Thousands of men in history haved attempted to change themselves or society in an effort to try and achieve something approaching a balance of power between men and women. They have failed, they have been ridiculed and taunted, tortured, killed and ignored, but they have never given up. They have often been deeply misguided, but, what I want to make clear is, they didn't start doing all this in 1988, when the *Daily Mail* first noticed. There is a history behind it, a long and complex history of which I would like to give a thumb-nail sketch.

Saint Cloud Man

In the tiny Loire valley settlement of Saint Cloud sur Didier in France there is a well-established wine merchants. Monsieur Horace Perpignnon is the *patron* of the establishment which was founded in the early eleventh century. One of the reasons for its longevity is the access the building has to a cave. This is used for wine storage and due to the peculiar rock formations and weather conditions it maintains a constant temperature all the year round, perfect for the long-term storage of wine.

The caves are well known locally; what is less well known, however, is that behind the wine racks, on the curved walls of the ancient rock, there are cave paintings of astonishing detail and significance.

They were first documented in 1840 by Professor Jacques Montinard who was a specialist in ancient history at the Sorbonne in Paris. Unfortunately, due to the attitudes prevalent at the time and Professor Montinard's own problems with his masculinity,* he decided that the paintings were of only minor importance and they were lost to us for over a hundred years.

In 1968 Monsieur Perpignnon's son, Phillipe, wanted to turn the caves into a Baba Cool† club. His father was opposed to it, but was brow-beaten by his wife, who was transferring the love she did not receive from her husband on to her son. A fairly classic situation, but not entirely relevant to the story. As Phillipe started to do up the cave, he came across the paintings, and thankfully, did not cover them up with peace symbols and badly carried out renditions of Asterix and Obelix. Now the paintings are protected and have been analysed by specialists from all over the world.

What they clearly show, as we can see, is that Saint Cloud man was not the traditional cave man we have been mythologically led to believe in. He was not going out hunting for food and killing other men, then dragging women off by the hair. The paintings show him weaving beads, making love gifts for women, in one rendition we can clearly see him caring for the young, sweeping the cave with what looks like a primitive broom, and also, most surprising of all, protecting animals. One image clearly shows a man protecting a wild boar from being speared by a woman hunter, which can only lead us to believe that there was an argument going on within the domestic scene

* Professor Montinard was married seven times, each time to women much younger than him. At the age of eighty-three he married a fourteen-year-old servant girl but, thankfully for her, he died before the marriage was consummated.

† Hippy.

even at this early stage on the presence of high saturated fat contents in the family diet.

Saint Cloud man shows us something far more important though. There is nothing new. Struggles between men and women have changed shape, size and colour over the millennia, but fundamentally we have already been through all the various stances and procedures many times as a species. The difference this time may be that we are aware of this, and yet still continue the struggle.

The Story of Cwbriogha

The ancient Irish Folk tale, Cwbriogha,* part of the rich Celtic oral tradition, has been told around evening fires for centuries. Recent re-interpretation of the original Gaelic tale has given a new light to the story.

Traditionally it was believed to tell the tale of a warrior who fell out with his King and went on a journey where he met a Princess from a neighbouring kingdom. He raced her on foot while she rode bareback on a pair of crazed

* The only contemporary translation we have for the ancient Celtic name Cwbriogha is Darren.

stallions. He won the race, won her heart and won the kingdom.

Now, a new translation by a team at Dublin University gives a different interpretation. They claim it tells the story of Cwbriogha, a man who was cast out of his village when the elders found him doing 'a woman's work'. He was apparently cooking and looking after his three children while his wife, Dinnasmaioghy, was sick.

What seemed to upset the village elders more than anything was that Cwbriogha seemed happy in his role in what we would now classify as 'chief carer'. The menfolk told him that if he kept on doing this, the crops would fail, the children would die and their whole way of life would come to an end. Cwbriogha did not agree with them.

Late one night the elders of the village came to see him, to confront him with their disquiet. It is said he crowned one with a mighty log and ran another through with his sword before mounting his horse and riding off into the night. This is an interesting detail, as it is quite clear he was anything but a wimp. In fact, in all the interpretations of the original story, he is known for being a bull of a man who was not averse to drinking, fighting and stabbing pigs through the heart with his finger.

Cwbriogha then leads a life of travel and adventure, but all through his hair-rising exploits there are mentions of his moments of tenderness, his abilities in the culinary and domestic fields, his knowledge of herbs, methods of drying lichen for use as a sponge during a woman's menses, his abilities to communicate with very young children and his unstoppable desire to 'tidy up'. After a particularly bloody battle it is said Cwbriogha

> did pick up all the swords and make them into a pile. He

> then gathered shields, making one pile of enemy ones, and one of his King's. The bodies of the slain were likewise sorted, and buried. After a day's hard labour on the battle field, Cwbriogha had made it so no man could tell that he had slain two hundred men there. It was spotless.*

This does tend to show that perhaps men were questioning their roles from as far back as 11 AD which is when mythology specialists estimate Cwbriogha would have existed. It could also suggest that the roles we now see as 'normal' or traditional ones for men, are in fact fairly recent inventions. For all we know, Cwbriogha could have been archetypical in his peer group, a completely normal man who just happened to have a bit of a temper. It is all theory, we shall never know.

Christians

Early Christian males were often persecuted not for their religious beliefs as many people believe, but because of their rather more, as we would see it now, 'aware' attitudes toward the position of women in society and the home, and the role men have played in their oppression. I want to underline here that I am talking about early Christian males, the sort that got eaten by lions in front of thousands of Romans in what must have been an extraordinary primal

* This is taken from *The Myth of Cwbriogha, Mad Axe Man or Gentle Carer?* written by Professor Alan Gore and Dr Randy Blimey, published by Treewood Press at £17.99.

sexual atmosphere. I am not referring to the later varieties of Christian males who took it upon themselves to oppress women in quite horrifyingly brutal ways for two thousand years, vestiges of whom still raise their ugly voices to attempt to pass mysoginist judgement to this day.

It is a little known fact that in Rome at this time, the term Christian had a very similar cultural meaning as the words *wimp, pouf, sissy, nancy boy, ladies' man* and *smarmy git* would have today. Masculinity, as we now understand it, was being consolidated during this period, marble statue by marble statue. The struggle to contain and crush the gentle, softer side of the gender was well under way; anything seen to challenge this was of course a direct threat to the strength and power of the empire.

Not only did Roman men feel Christians might open up emotional doors within their hearts, they were very concerned about the response some of the better educated Roman women were portraying. According to Cicero and others, from writings in their private diaries, Christians with their soft eyes, gentle smile and modest ways were seen as trying to butter up women.*

This greatly disturbed Roman males, who being emotionally blocked due to their brutalised upbringings and military training,† were incapable of anything approaching gentleness or humility. It is thought some

* Cicero Apolonius wrote in his journal of 102 AD, 'Today at the Market of Adropolinus I spied a Christian smiling benignly upon a young maiden, who, so taken by his countenance, did go with him thence unto a place he called a Temple. I feel it is her Temple he will be entering before long. I pondered on why the young maid did not look at me, in all my Roman finery, but at the ragged Christian.'

† So clearly a precursor to the training of Fascist soldier males in Germany of the 30s and 40s.

women went as far as to suggest that their Roman men could 'learn a thing or two from those semi-naked Christian fellows'.

The classic Roman male response to a challenge to his superiority from a lesser male was to kill him, hence the lions, the seething crowds and the heady sexual chaos of witnessing disembowelment at the fangs of a beast.*

The 'Victorian' New Man

I will deal with the term 'new man' later in the book, but interestingly the following extract from *The Times* carries what I believe to be the first use of the term. It was printed in May 1878.

> Sir,
>
> It is with dismay I hear of the traitorous behaviour of my own sex as regards the activities of these ghastly harridan suffragette war maidens. As if life weren't bad enough having screaming harpies dogging one's steps at every opportunity, we are now witness to the antics of her spineless and hen pecked brother. He hides behind her petty-coats, hoping we menfolk will not see him, braying at us sickeningly. This new man is a sorry sight indeed.
>
> Is he trying to prove to these women who would be men that he is less of a man than they? Does he think he will gain some advantage in so doing, some sweet favour

* The sexuality of witnessing human consumption by wild animals has been explored in unimaginable detail in the book *Oral Death, The Eroticism of Bestial Mastication*, by Huupter Von Gregerhoffman, published by Zugger und Zugger, Hamburg.

from them? I can for the life of me see no other reason.

I am sure sir, you will agree with me this new man should be treated in the strictest possible way. A sound thrashing might knock some sense into him.

Yours, etc. etc.

Sir N. Forceforth

As we can see here, there is nothing new about the new man. The men Sir Neave Forceforth* is referring to supported the women's suffrage movement and modern principles such as free health care for children and the provision of birth control clinics accessible to all women.

These activities were, naturally, seen to be undermining the very fabric of society, and any man who admitted having any sympathy with such views was instantly deemed 'new' or wet as we would now understand it. The arguments raged for many months in *The Times* and other publications.

The new men of this period were perhaps, it is true, the ultimate male apologists. From photographs of the period we can see that they felt immensely guilty, but also fancied fiery suffragette women and must have gone through tortures of guilt and denial which are hard to imagine in contemporary times. They were very sincere, and tried hard to find a way to fit in with the struggles which were going on around them. It is hard for us to judge them now, but from contemporary accounts, they all sound rather stiff. It wasn't until the beginning of the twentieth century,

* Sir Neave Forceforth was a member of the City of London council from 1860 until 1887. He was a self-made man, whose wealth was founded on uncertain trades and business. He had a reputation for being a family man, a strict moralist and a stern task master, 'cruel but fair' was how one grovelling sycophant described him. He was married with eleven children and died in a brothel on the Mile End Road in 1887.

when notions of 'free love' started to circulate, that a lot of these men would start to deal with their own sexuality in anything even approaching a healthy manner.

Non-Aligned Anarcho-Syndicalists

This was an obscure group of mainly British and German intellectuals who thrived from the turn of the century to the early thirties. They formed 'commonwealth' communities in rural areas, a famous one in this country being the Combe Bank Colony near Taunton in Devon. The reason behind this isolationist policy came from the feeling that their behaviour did not 'fit in' with normal society where they were clearly feared and mistrusted.

They therefore built their own houses and lived in self-supporting, non-competitive, non-ownership-based commonwealths. They wore strange clothes: the women sometimes wore trousers, the men often wore their hair long and walked around in sandals or 'Jerusalem boots' as they came to be known. But most shocking was the fear that they did odd things with each other. At least that is how they were portrayed by outsiders.

They practised 'free love'. Partnerships between men and women based on freedom, love and a total lack of ownership. The man did not consider any woman partner to be his chattel – she could come and go as she pleased. So could he. It was a brave attempt to find an idyllic way for men and women to live together. Needless to say, it had its drawbacks.

Frankson Haptchik was a writer who lived on the

Combe Bank Colony as a boy during the First World War, and then as an adult until he left in 1928. He recalls how things operated in his book, *Freedom and Cabbages, Life at the Combe Bank Colony*, which was published in 1932.

This extract is from the book:

> Edith came around that night in tears. She had been fighting with Percy all day. He had thrown one of his sculptures through the window. This was the last straw for poor Edith, their house was in a bad state as it was. It had been mentioned at commonwealth meetings, but Percy would simply curse them for being 'lily livered' and storm out. I held Edith for many hours as she sobbed, and we ended up making love in the cold morning light. I was woken after only a few minutes' sleep by Gerald, who reminded me I was on carrot digging duty that morning. I tried to make excuses, but obviously Gerald was at the end of this tether as Mary was clearly spending more time with Horace who had built an extension on to his house so he could be with which ever women he desired and desired him, and not leave Harriet. Everyone except the children knew that Harriet was a friend of Dorothy,* so didn't worry too much.
>
> I dug the carrots. Gerald said he was going to leave and join the army. He felt that the military may have drawbacks, but at least they were honest about what they did. Kill people. Although it would be very much against commonwealth policy to agree with him, I could see his point.

Despite the complications depicted above, the notion of free love was a very popular one around this time. In 1922 in the United States a man called Gilwood Hinchcliff, a

* Lesbian.

writer, thinker and practitioner of free love, wrote *The Bed of Chains*,* which was a powerful indictment of modern marriage. In it he claimed that both men and women were trapped by the institution of marriage, and until women were set free from it, no man would be free. He felt that women were more trapped by it, but he was trying to make his argument appeal to a male readership. He used the example of wives and mistresses, claiming that the latter were always more fun to be with than the former. His feelings of bitterness at the behaviour a woman adopted as soon as she became a wife seeps through every line, and the obvious joy he felt at having illicit relationships with women half his age is barely contained. He did acknowledge that men had the better deal, because society, which he claimed was 'male dominated' accepted that men were allowed to have relationships with 'mistresses'.

Hinchcliff was married to a Russian poet called Ellyenka Rapostovnia Distrova Vonyovonko Kyritznialyoznia† at the time the book was published. Ellyenka was his second wife. His first, a dancer by the name of Lilly Tantrum, had committed suicide by jumping off the Brooklyn Bridge in 1915 with a fifty-five pound lump hammer tied to her neck.

Ellyenka was not too pleased by what she read in Hinchcliff's book. She thought that, although free love could theoretically liberate the masses, deception of the people you love was another form of oppression. Hinchcliff defended himself by claiming that all people must be free

* *The Bed of Chains* published by Jacobs & Binkovitz, New York, 1922. The book is a personal account of Gilwood Hinchcliff's life and loves. His cheating, his double standards, hypocrisy and self-aggrandisement make hysterical reading with the benefit of hindsight. Boy did those guys take themselves seriously.

† She was published under the name of Elly Walker after advice from her agent.

and if her love for him couldn't climb the small hill of his infidelities, then she wasn't worth knowing.

He had always wanted them to have an 'open marriage' which Ellyenka claimed meant that he could make love with any women he chose, and she should stay at home and look after the children. Hinchcliff disagreed with this, always assuring her it would work both ways. However, when he discovered she had been seeing another man, he apparently went berserk, almost tearing their Long Island beach front weather-board house down to its foundations. Three muscle-bound homosexual fishermen had to pin him down to stop his disassembling the entire neighbourhood.

Three years later Ellyenka had also committed suicide,* and Hinchcliff married for a third time, this time a very timid preacher's daughter from Kansas. His famous quote at his third and final marriage ceremony was 'One artist in the family is quite enough thank you.'

Interestingly, for a man who devoted the first half of his life to 'liberating' people from the shackles of post-Victorian morals, Gilwood Hinchcliff ended up on a Senate committee which was looking at ways of rounding up homosexuals into concentration camps and removing the right to vote from women, teachers and Jews. He died, alone and an alcoholic in 1956. His last wife is still alive and living with another woman in a lovely, though slightly battered wooden house on the beach on Long Island.

* She blew her brains out on stage at a poetry reading attended by some very influential people. This event appeared in over sixty novels written at about that time, the most famous being *The Confusion of Mirrors and Windows* by Phillip Wallace, which was developed into the Bertrand Bluvier film, *Lovely Long Dresses* starring Dianne Keaton and Charlie Sheen.

Conchies

Conchies, or conscientious objectors, were men who for moral, religious and personal reasons decided that they couldn't join in the national war effort during the last two world wars. Some were sent to prison for their beliefs, many did vital war work away from the front line, and some particularly brave ones became medics and orderlies with various Red Cross organisations and religious medical services.

Often men of great integrity, bravery and moral conviction, they were naturally treated like shit by the average Tommy. 'Wet liberal, lily-livered sissies and nancy boys with a yellow streak a mile wide all down their back, probably foreign who would have no problem driving Italian tanks*', would be how our brave boys described them.

What in fact we may have been looking at was the precursor of the ultra right-on man. This phenomenon, which only really came into being during the mid-eighties, was a type of figure who would not compromise on any point. An ultra hard-line – one could almost say Stalinist – attitude to personal politics, the environment and sexuality.

The 'conchie' was the man who would not compromise his views and opinions no matter what the cost, the old equivalent to the Animal Rights activist, the staunch

* Italian tanks were supposed to have one forward gear and six reverse. The Italian army were known to have surrendered in droves at the first sign of a fight. This is of course completely ignoring the bravery of the many thousands of men and women who resisted the rule of fascism in Italy in the 30s and 40s and who gave their lives in their thousands in order to liberate their fellow countrymen. Typical bit of re-writing of history, but what can you do?

vegetarian who would willingly go to prison in order to release a couple of chain-smoking beagles and a rabbit.*

These men set the pace in many ways: they are the butt of cruel jokes, they will suffer the taunts of people who consider themselves wiser, saner. They are easy targets, standing there in their vegen shoes and funny haircuts, eating weird pulses and grains, talking obsessively about which type of bladderwort contains vitamin B12. There you go you see, I'm doing it. But only a few years ago, anyone who re-cycled a jam jar was considered some sort of nutter. Now look at every Safeway car park. Re-cyclers' heaven. The most middle-of-the-road, suburban house-husband has an array of boxes under the sink, one for newspapers and magazines, one for glass, one for plastic etc.

In Australia there are about eight different dustmen or garbos who take away different rubbish items which are then graded and re-cycled. This is big business, but as recently as the mid seventies you couldn't really say re-cycled unless you had long hair and had lived in a nude sculptors' commune outside Amsterdan.

However, conchies were certainly part of the seedbed of the modern reconstructured man, a cornerstone in the process.

* People may read a note of disdain into my opinion of such activity. In no way do I mean to imply this – I have the greatest respect for such people. I just think it's always worth remembering that in this country we have the *Royal* Society for the Prevention of Cruelty to Animals, and only the *National* Society for the Prevention of Cruelty to Children.

Ladies' Men

From one point of view, I am dealing with an historical string of so-called villains here, dating back to pre history. All the men I have referred to are seen as a threat to masculinity: to upstanding, emotionally blocked men who have ruled the earth so ruthlessly for so long.

One of the most despised, and often most misunderstood images was that of 'the ladies' man'. Often portrayed in films as 'only after one thing' these cravat-wearing smoothies were loathed for their 'clever ways with a girl'.

The erotically hopeless English men of the 40s and 50s felt that a ladies' man* was, apart from being more socially capable with women, likely to 'take their girl away', show her 'slimy' tricks and she would never come back to him.

There may indeed have been an element of truth in these feelings. English men of the period were known to be the most sexually retarded on the planet at that time.

This was of course partly due to the war, but mainly due to the collapse of empire and the feeling of emasculation that many men went through. They tried to bolster this up with beer drinking, chain smoking, back slapping, camaraderie type behaviour which soon became entrenched as 'normal'.† The ladies' man would have none of this, and was consequently easy to spot.

* There was always an unspoken fear that a ladies' man might have been 'foreign' in some way. French and Italian men were often seen as ladies' men, Germans on the other hand, were not. This may be something to do with the way French and Italian men are brought up, i.e. not to see women as 'the enemy' but as possible friends and lovers. German men at this time, as we all know, had a pathological fear of women.

† I see this period as the time of the emergence of the 'normal' man, who I will deal with in greater detail later.

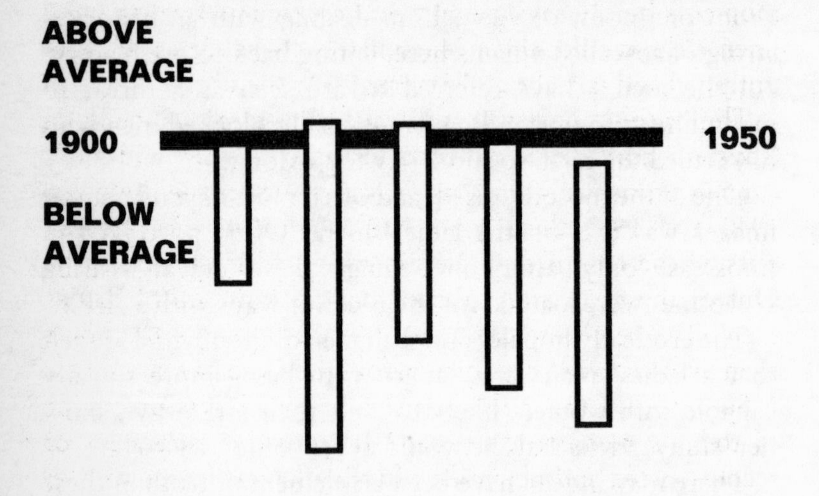

For a start, due to his wealth and connections he would wear comfortable, or possibly even nice looking clothes, as opposed to the war-time utility clothing which made all men look like convicts. He would have time to listen to women, understand their worries and dislikes, he would not swagger about and try to impress her with sad displays of his masculinity.

And, just as the boys in the pub feared, he was an expert and sensitive lover. Many women found that ladies' men were far more open about themselves and their feelings, far easier to talk to after a session of sexual congress, and most importantly of all, far less hung-up about their mothers. They could make love for hours in ways which women liked, not too much light, not too much dirty talk, and only the occasional cigarette between positions.

By contrast a woman would find the normal man of the period able to sustain an erection for only a matter of moments before saying sorry and coming all over the bed linen. He would then immediately light up a Players untipped and talk about darts, rugby or the war.

The ladies' man was portrayed in films as being a 'shyster'. Someone who 'got a girl into trouble' and did a runner. Statistically this has proved to be untrue. Between 1940 and 1960 there were 370,000 pregnancies created outside the confines of the marriage bed in this country. Out of these, 23 were blamed on the activities of 'ladies men'. The rest were the fault of 'normal men' who didn't even make it to the bed linen before they said 'sorry'.*

So who was the ladies' man? Is he possibly a precursor of today's reconstructed man? It's possible that a lot of reconstructed and new men of today have a father who in the past once wore a navy blue blazer, a paisley cravat, cavalry twill trousers, a tweed jacket and soft brown suede shoes. The sort of Terry Thomas figure whose eyes lit up when he spied a beautiful woman, whose lips pursed involuntarily, who sucked air in through his teeth making a rather unpleasant hissing sound, and managed to make the word '*hello*' last four seconds.

* The use of the word 'sorry' as a warning for an approaching male ejaculation is looked at in more detail in the sex section. That's the bit that's already been thumbed and made grubby near the end. Don't worry, you'll find it.

chapter 2
Definitions

Over the last twenty years we have witnessed a few fairly major changes in some advanced Western societies. Chief amongst these has been the impact of the 'women's movement'. There are more women in more positions of power in more countries now, than there have ever previously been in recorded history. This is of course not to say that the struggle is over – far from it; but there has been some change. In contrast to this series of changes, one of the smallest discernible sociological shifts in history has been as a result of these changes, i.e. the male response to the women's movement.

The Emergence of the Reconstructed Heart

As the eighties blended into the nineties many people*

* And when I say people, I mean women. This is an attempt to reverse the assumed male gender tag of the word 'people'. If you think about it, you probably saw a man, or group of men when you read the word 'people', but now you're reading this footnote you will no doubt take offence at my attempt to trick you as it were, and deny to yourself and others that this was ever the case.

started to realise that although society had seen huge changes in behaviour, work patterns* and domestic responsibility, very little had changed as regards male attitudes and outlook. In some ways those people were correct, but I wanted to look in detail at what had happened. I have examined attitudes and behaviour amongst a very small, select group of men in this country.†

The men I worked with came mainly from a middle class, moderately well educated background and were generally of a liberal to soft left political disposition.‡ Because of what has happened to them, and what they have done to themselves, I have come to classify them as men who had in some way been reconstructed.

They were not born ready kitted out with any divine form of awareness, in many cases far from it. They were brought up in an environment just the same as any man, but through their early sexual lives became unhappy with what were the accepted, or 'normal' male attitudes.

They didn't want to be macho men, they didn't want to be wimps. They didn't want to be sulking footballers who apologise as they reach orgasm, or bespectacled intellectuals whose genitalia have shrivelled through lack of use. They wanted to be 'different' to the men who went before. They had a hard job. There was a dire shortage of role models, so many of these men have created proto, or inner role models. Fictitious 'dream men' who they could base

* By 1988 72% of women in this country were working full or part time. This means the number of women who are 'housewives' in the traditional sense is down in the low 5-7%.

† I have to be specific here as I am dealing with what could be the leading edge, the *avant-garde* if you like, of socio-economic change. I am not dealing with the huge majority of men, as will soon become apparent.

‡ This is another area I will look at later. A certain shift to the right is discernible in some quarters.

themselves on. This type of behaviour is of course fraught with dangers but it was an interesting area and one I wanted to look at in detail.

The results were often quite startling, I was looking at a group of men who had completely rid themselves of the shackles and blinkers of their forefathers and appear to have emerged as a new breed. More whole, more gentle, stronger, more forceful, their chins stuck out a little more with non-arrogant sensitive determination.

For a while I was convinced. I thought they had found the new way forward, the path along which, some time in the future, the goal of true equality between the genders lay. The question I am going to attempt to answer is, was I right?

What Does Reconstruction Mean?

Reconstruction should in no way be confused with reform. From the early part of this century onwards, people of a liberal disposition tried to reform social inequality. The motivation behind this drive seems to be guilt. Comfortable middle class people saw poor people and thought 'it was a terrible shame'. Terms like 'something's got to be done!' were bandied about at warm, well-fed dinner tables all over the country.

The reformers felt guilty but never became *revolutionaries* because they felt society was basically good and they didn't want to fiddle with things too much. It could all get dreadfully messy, possibly even violent, and for reformers, any display of emotion was a little unpleasant. They had nice houses and servants, their clothes were cheap because the cotton came from India and was woven in Halifax. India and Halifax were full of poor people. The battle cry 'something's got to be done!' obviously had a subtext which was 'but not too much because I like being able to afford lots of nice shirts'.

They didn't really want to change anything, they just wanted to make it a bit less obviously painful for poor people. They had a conscience, so when they saw a poor person cough themselves to death in a wet street, it spoiled their enjoyment.

Reconstruction, on the other hand, is a more profound and far-reaching process. It can in many ways be more closely linked with revolution. Many revolutionary governments around the world have proclaimed a period of 'reconstruction' for their country, before grinding the populace into the dust in order to pay for arms sold to them by the West.

But inner reconstruction, which is what I'm dealing with here, doesn't follow the tenets of Marx or Engels, in fact it doesn't follow anyone's tenets because there are none to follow. Inner reconstruction is a whole new ball game.

In order to understand what is going on we need to step outside the workings of the human mind and use marvellous 'olde worlde' story-telling techniques.* Over my years of work on the subject I have discovered that a good way to think about it and understand the process of reconstruction is to imagine a man as a large run-down inner city house.

In my mind's eye this house is in an area of north

* I originally learned about these while attending a 'weekend intensive' in Tenessee, sitting in a sweat lodge for thirty hours with a dozen huge American men. All nude. Quite shocking at first but it's amazing what you can get used to.

London, fashionable a hundred years ago, but by the early seventies, after the ravages of the war and developers, run down and in disrepair. I have visited equivalent areas around the world, Manchester, Liverpool, Glasgow, Sydney, Melbourne, Chicago, New York. In fact most large cities in the developed world.*

So, back to the analogy. There's our house, standing in the rain, looking a little battered. In 1970 the last tenants moved out and it looked like the end, the house would remain empty for ever, it was due for demolition to make way for a ten-lane spur road to feed a nearby elevated urban highway. Due to the levels of corruption and old boy back-slapping in local planning departments, this never came to fruition. The house remained empty and unloved, a cold wind blew through the gaps in the brickwork.

Then, in 1972, politically motivated squatters moved in and formed a commune. They did some low-level maintenance, they painted the walls bright colours but fundamentally they left the structure of the building untouched. However, it did look a happier place in which to live. The toilets worked, there were pot plants in the windows. Old rugs pulled from building skips adorned the floors. Basic funiture filled the rooms. There were parties and people sat around saying things like 'mad magic man', 'let's build a windmill', and 'pass me that Umma Gumma album cover and I'll put one together'.

So here we have masculinity *circa* 1973 – post-sixties, supposedly softer and more open. But was a change really

* Except Vancouver which was perfect when it was built and has remained perfect, and everyone who lives there is perfect and they all have a perfect lifestyle (except native Americans whose life is shit). I even saw a tramp there, jogging between garbage cans in a pair of trainers.

taking place? If it wasn't, the world around certainly was.

By 1975 the next-door house had become a strictly run vegetarian wholefood co-op. It was run by people who frowned on late night take-away food after the pub. Bacon sandwiches and sausage and mash were considered counter-revolutionary, the food of the oppressor. The co-op attracted people from all over the world, and they all had an influence on it and the houses they came into contact with. People fleeing from Chile, Nicaragua and El Salvador brought stories of real suffering with them as they weighed out the pulses and tofu. Realism was being faced within the house, it caused friction, but there was no turning back.

Another key factor in the slow dawning of consciousness* in the house took place when another neighbouring house was used as one of the first rape crisis centres. It was a women only house with strict security at all times. No longer was it possible to climb over the wall at the back and 'bum some tea bags'. Arguments raged over what involvement a man could have, there were many lumps in throats as well-meaning men were turned away, not even allowed to do the hoovering. There was much discussion at this time about the relevance of Indian wall hangings and candles. 'Troops Out' posters started to appear in communal hallways, lots of screen printed clenched fists with Italian writing underneath would adorn the upstairs loo. At Christmas a poster was hung on the door under the holly. It read, 'Three wise *men*? You must be joking.'

Was it possible the house was learning the language of the new thought, making the outward signs that it had

* This was a very popular term around this time. Everything was considered to have a consciousness, especially someone you fancied. You would often 'love their consciousness'.

changed, or had it really shifted its focus? It was still too early to tell.

In 1979 the area started to look up. Due to the victory of the Thatcher government and the explosion of activity in the financial markets, inner city areas suddenly looked a lot more attractive to the investor with a bit of imagination.

In September of that year a dentist bought the house for what would later be thought of as an astonishingly small amount of money. He kept the flower boxes and the *Atomkraft Nein Danke* sticker in the window, he hung non exploitative Afghan curtains and he lined the walls with a truly phenomenal collection of books by women writers.

The rooms were comfortable and welcoming, the space was completely re-designed, all the walls featured softened edges, you could feel the effort the house was making. It was really trying hard. Particular attention was paid to the bathroom, but above all, this house gave good kitchen.

Later still, in the mid-eighties now, after surveyors' reports which pointed out the structural faults of the old building, the house was completely gutted from attic to basement. The exterior walls were shored up with scaffolding and the entire house was rebuilt inside. New floors, walls, heating and lighting ducts and an underground garage were installed. The decorative layers chosen with such care in the 70s were peeled off exposing the raw brickwork and structural beams. When it was finally finished, the house was lean, mean and moody looking. Matt black furniture replaced the old mish mash of styles. Terence Conran's influence could be felt all over. The floors were all of polished birds eye maple, imported from Canada, the doors were bomb proof laminate from Sweden. The kitchen, an extraordinary display of shades of grey, was mainly Neff, with a few lumpy herb dishes from North Africa and Provence. One of the basement rooms, which had once been used to print the underground magazine, *Street Warrior*, was now a mini gymnasium. The house was more attractive than its seventies version. However some people claimed that what it had gained in style, it had lost in soul.

That said, you cannot tell what changes a house has undergone merely by looking at the facade. When choosing a house or a man, you need to know if the *interior* has been reconstructed. You need to know if he has a reconstructed heart.

Notes on 'The Study Group'

From time to time I will include quotes from what I call my study group. Due to the fact that some of my work has taken place at the obscure end of the pop psychology spectrum I think I should explain what I mean by this.

My study group is a loose knit collection of men I have worked with over the past twenty years. They range in age from 20 to 73, and in income from the low tens to the upper hundreds of thousands* per year. I don't want readers to get the wrong impression and think that these men all sat around in a disused primary school on a Saturday morning, took their shoes off and had a group weep. I would generally interview them on their own territory and the wearing of shoes was entirely up to them.

They are also not all reconstructed. I have defined four

* I'm talking sterling here, for those of you wondering.

main categories: reconstructed men, the area I am looking at in most detail, self-loathing men, defensive men and 'normal men'. When I use a quote I will usually introduce the speaker and make it clear in which category I have classed him.

I have obviously held careful discussions on the use of definitions; the very act of putting human beings into categories is fraught with danger. Popular music groups such as Pink Floyd built whole careers around making crass right-wing libertarian statements about such things as being trapped in a pigeon hole. In fact it's quite surprising one of their concerts didn't feature a 200-foot-long inflatable pigeon breaking free from some polystyrene box. However, I digress. I have taken great care to make my pigeon holes as specific as possible, but the section on normal men is the one that has aroused the most controversy, expecially with my European colleagues.

They claim that what I classify as a universal 'normal' man is in fact a super-typical British man, and that an average unreconstructed Frenchman, Belgian, Italian or German would have a wholly different set of attitudes and behavioural symptoms to the ones I describe.

I can see they have a point, so it may well be worth remembering while reading the section on normal men that most, but certainly not all, of the normal members of my study group were of Anglo Saxon or Celtic stock. I have obviously not made any reference to anyone's ethnic background, because we all have prejudices, one way or the other, even if we are super liberals.

I didn't want to allow any normal man reading the book to be able to nod to himself and say, 'Well, I might be sexist and emotionally blocked, but I'm not as bad as ...' whereupon he fills in his least favourite ethnic sub group.

I hope that has cleared up the question of prejudice.

Why Now?

If not now, when? as the saying goes. Many people have asked me if I know why there is now a sudden interest in 'men', or 'the men issue'. Why not ten, or twenty years ago?

In the last twenty years women have transformed their lives but have paid a high price. They have slowly taken power in public life, but have been burdened with responsibilities in private. To all intents and purposes, men haven't changed at all, and they are going to have to. And it's not just a question of domestic labour, it goes far deeper, into ever corner of our lives.

As women have been entering the workplace, they have commented on the obvious shortfalls in men's lives: male inability to communicate on anything other than a technical level being a prime example. It might be expected that these huge sociological changes might influence male attitudes to some extent, but as we can see, the evidence of this gulf between expectation and result clearly points to no discernible change.

This graph (statistics gleaned from a huge world survey commissioned by the United Nations Emotional Evaluation Committee)* shows that women have not exactly

* U.N.E.E.C. was set up in 1983 to try to regulate world-wide fluctuations in emotional feelings as a means of controlling international conflict.

been spoilt for choice when it comes to emotionally open and aware male partners.

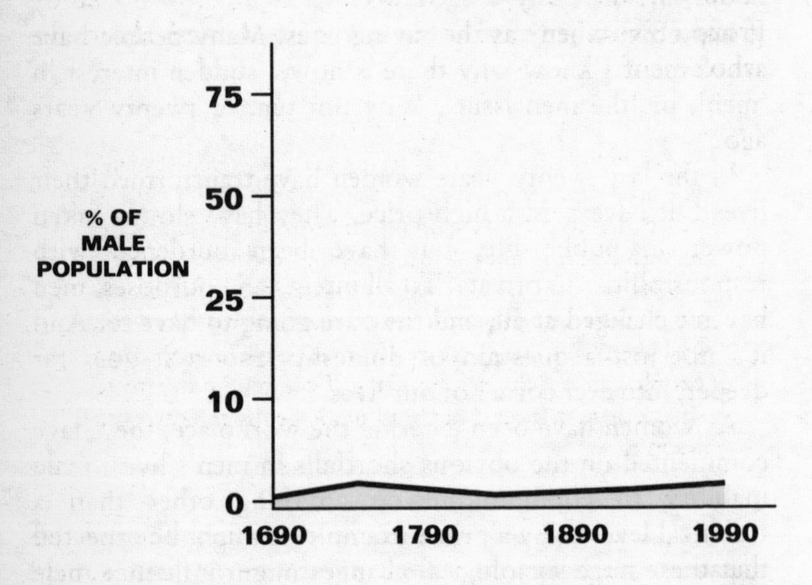

Another glaring example of men's failure to change: although shifting work patterns over the last twenty years have meant that the majority of women now work, advertising executives* have only just picked up on the fact that words like 'housewife' went out of date in late 1958.

* Executives meaning male. Although a lot of women work in the advertising industry, the people in power are men, as are the clients. They love to use terms like 'the housewife' in interviews; in private they will use terms like, 'a right Tracy' or 'a total Sharon' when describing a social type they are aiming their marketing strategy at.

in the early 90s they are just beginning to update their language. Women have changed, men are just beginning to notice.

There has also been, as I have already stated, a rather obvious lack of role models for men to say, 'If I was like him, I wouldn't be a sexist git or a wet wimp'. I talked about this difficulty with terms to a member of my study group, Simon Greatrex. He got quite heated about the whole issue.

> We only have the dreadful terms such as 'feminist man', or 'non-sexist man' as if anyone wants to be one of those. They're a contradiction in terms by definition. A feminist man is like saying a 'benign dictatorship' or a 'vegetarian butcher'. It's a joke and it really gets on my tits. Likewise with 'non sexist man', that's like 'non violent assault rifle'. It really makes me angry when people call me the wrong thing, I see red and want to smack them in the mouth, but I'm too gentle and caring so I don't.

This lack of positive role models, and the all-too apparent plethora of violent, rapist, sexist and super-aggressive role models which young boys learn to idolise from a young age, has meant that anything other than a negative response to women's changing roles has been difficult to find.

Interestingly enough there are five men who claim to be 'non-sexist'. They have each been through an enormous amount of psycho-, group and intensive therapy, they have discovered their inner wild man, they've been to marathon nude drumming sessions, they've been re-birthing, rolfing, weeping, bonding and raging, they are so completely re-built, re-shaped and reconstructed that even calling them human is stretching a point.

Due to the very nature of the process they have been through they have no desire for cheap publicity and therefore refused to grant me any interviews, yet again reducing the number of role models. They were very supportive of the work I was trying to do, although slightly mistrustful of the rather cheap, garish and public way in which I was doing it. They thought a book was a bit 'showy' and would have preferred a small pamphlet.

They wished me to point out however, that all of them are devoted to deeply committed, long-term, child-bearing, relationships with women of astonishing feminist credentials.*

This whole discussion is based on a search for terms. What do we call men who are slightly different, and what do we call the men they are slightly different from, and how do we define the difference? I will attempt to do that in the next section.

Normal Men

The very act of putting the words 'normal' and 'man' in the same sentence is, of course, a dangerous generalisation. However it is a commonly used term, the word 'Normal' coming from the Old French, Norman, meaning a warring peasant who was installed as landed gentry after the 'Norman' conquest of 1066.

* Except Jerry Barlow. Gorgeous looking man, single, heterosexual, lives at 26 Milner Park Road, Nottingham in case you're interested.

They have effectively lorded it over Anglo Saxons for a thousand years and careful study of the names of the rich and powerful in England will identify the predominance of Norman roots. The word normal has, due to this cultural hegemony,* become a generally accepted basis of measurement.†

Considered by society to be healthy and well balanced, this sort of man operates with one part of his life completely ignored: his non-violent emotions. He is not generally willing to admit he has these, or any other emotions, until it is far too late. Therefore when some occurrence upsets him he has no idea why, and even less idea how to solve the problem.

One clear area of difference between him and reconstructed man is normal mans inability to communicate intimately with any other individuals, particularly other men. All emotional communication between normal males is done in strictly coded language. For instance if one man feels a strong bond of friendship with another he will call his friend a series of offensive names and hit him repeatedly about the shoulder and back area.‡

Nevertheless, even in the most ordered of male lives a crisis or disturbance will inevitably visit. It is impossible to deny the existence of strong emotional feelings. We all have them, but the normal man doesn't like them. He will do anything to avoid them by channelling the energy into

* Hegemony – meaning leadership or predominant authority – was a very trendy term in the late seventies and early eighties. Hunch-backed lefty men used to love talking about the 'cultural hegemony of the USA'. They could have said 'cultural imperialism', but I think they felt too many people might know what they were talking about. I discovered the best thing to do at times like this was to sit and nod a lot. Since then, expressions like 'I don't care what I'm supposed to think about politics and American stuff, I love it!' have become more popular.

† For more on this read *The Norman Yoke* by Roland Muldoon published by Hackney Empire Press.

‡ This sort of behaviour is most commonly practised by men who fall under the heading of 'Rugger Bugger'. That is men who have reached physical maturity but are still children emotionally and psychologically. According to a recent survey this state applies to over 73% of men in this country.

other areas. Researchers have found that fishing, heavy drinking, model railways, aggressive driving, frenetic masturbation and unprovoked violence are by far the most popular.

Popular Activities when Under Stress (Normal Men)

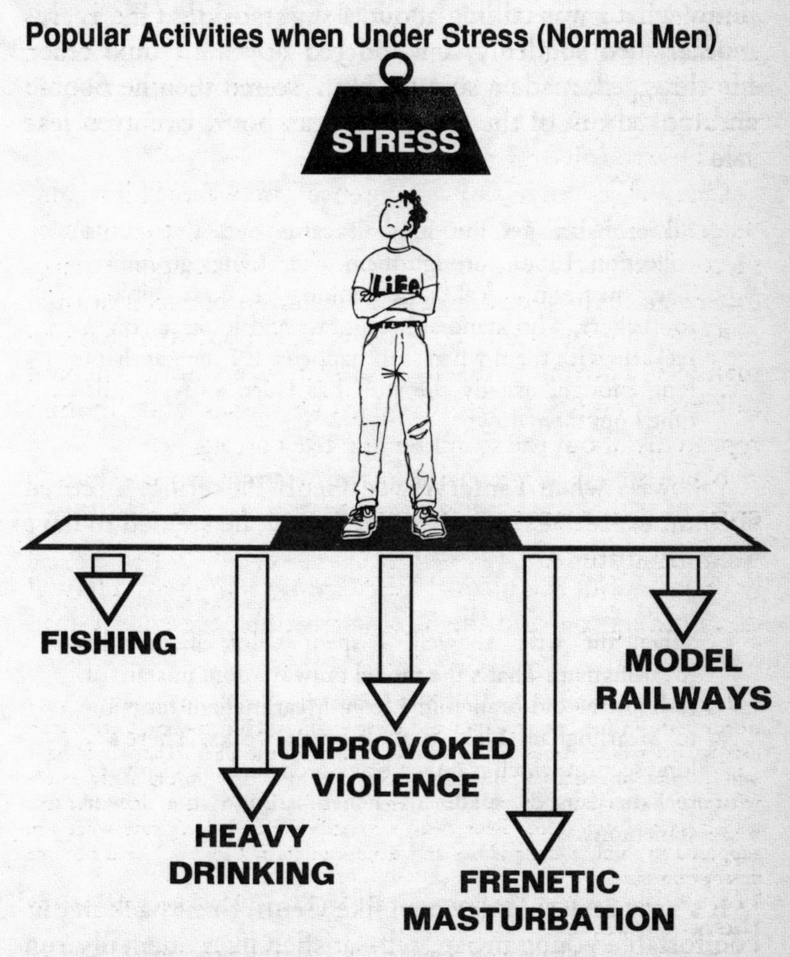

This type of avoidance behaviour can be very difficult for other members of the man's family or friends to deal with. Joe Maxwell a twenty-eight-year-old carpenter from Leicester is a member of my study group. He gave me some excellent examples of avoidance behaviour. When I asked him about avoidance technique he claimed he didn't know what I was talking about. I suggested that if, say, his mother died suddenly, I wondered how he would react. He shrugged, made a sort of 'Huh' sound then he pouted and looked out of the window for an hour. Eventually he said.

> I'd probably get my football cards out. I've got a collection. I look through them when things go funny. They make me feel safe, looking at these blokes, footballers, who stand still on grass and look at you. I feel safe with them when stuff happens. If I stare at them long enough, usually the stuff has faded away by the time I put them down.

Likewise when I interviewed Geoff Pickering, a retired account executive from Esher in Surrey, he seemed to have a similar attitude.

> When the wife ... well, I spent a lot of time in Mearlingham. That's the model railway room upstairs. I re-built the old branch line from Mearlingham Junction to Mearlingham Halt, it took seven weeks. There's a long section which is now a brick arch viaduct with very realistic bushes made of lichen around the lower stanchions.

It's very easy to judge men like Geoff, to sit back in our comfortable young urban, self-satisfied lives, mentally run through lists of our possessions and laugh, saying, 'what a sad old git'.

I admit I had to resist doing just that when I was interviewing him, but I remembered he was just behaving in what he considers a 'normal' way. Keeping his emotions firmly blocked and dammed in. He fears any relaxation from that will cause his boundaries to collapse and chaos to engulf him. It's all classic, classic blocked male behaviour.

I don't want to dwell on frenetic masturbation too much, although it is a very common phenomenon and certainly one that all men will have experienced at one time or another in their lives.

The myth seems to be that some men indulge in this activity when they are adolescents, the image of the teenage boy with the twenty-four-hour stiffy being a popular one in male mythology. But I am dealing with an older age group who will turn to this activity at times of emotional distress of decision making.

Geoff Pickering, who we met earlier, was eventually persuaded to explain why he finds the need to masturbate so much at certain times.

> I was shopping with Vera, the wife, and she asked me what sort of curtains we should have in the spare room. I don't know, I can't choose, there was all these different colours. I couldn't take it, so I went into the men's changing rooms, you know, where you try stuff on, and I had a wank. I just had to. Sometimes it's like that, like when our neighbour's kid got leukemia, and his mum was in our place crying. I couldn't listen so I went up to the bathroom, ran the taps and beat the bishop. I felt much better after.

Heavy drinking is another very popular way of avoiding the responsibilities that are part of being an adult male. Sadly it's reached epidemic proportions in many apparently advanced Western nations and there seems no sign of any change here. Bill Prescott from Walthamstow is a perfect example.

> As a rule I don't drink much, but if the missis starts giving me ear ache about love and that, I'm down the pub and getting ten pints inside me before you can say 'pissed as a rat'. I can't stand talking about stuff, like when she was attacked, I just turned me back on her and got pissed. Seemed like the best thing to do at the time. She's alright now, what's the bloody fuss about!*

The most common avoidance behaviour I have left until last. Violence, particularly unprovoked violence is a very worrying area and one which the average liberal has as little to do with as possible. Sudden street violence is very much the territory of the male, and although attacks on women are abhorrent and repulsive, it is in fact statistically far more likely for a man to be violently assaulted on the streets of our cities.

I interviewed a number of men who were serving at Her Majesty's pleasure in various establishments around the country. In one of these places I spoke to Trev; he's thirty-six, divorced and has a history of violent behaviour and involvement in violent crime going back to his days in a Nuneaton creche.

> It's a good way of getting rid of your anger, that's the way I've always looked at it. Like, once, this girl dumped me. I really loved her. And she just upped and left. So as she was telling me this, in a Wimpy bar in

* It was about this time Bill got a little aggressive and tried to make me swallow the tape recorder. Luckily I had a few cans of beer in the fridge and placated him with those.

> Colchester, as she was telling me, I was all riled up inside. I couldn't speak, so I went out the door. Saw this bloke walking along the street. I nutted him and kicked his head in. I don't know who he was, never seen him before, he was just there.

So, 'normal men' it seems, set the standard. These are the men that a reconstructed man can judge himself against. Normal behaviour is, by definition, anathema to a reconstructed man. He will always try to break out of those roles, or think about the problems facing him in a lateral way, not denying them, but dealing with them, in a hands on, emotionally mature and tactile manner. He will hug and bond his way through many problems that have been as a brick wall to his normal brothers and forebears. However, there are, as far as I can discern, two main stages which a man must travel through before progressing from normal to reconstructed. States known as defensive and self-loathing.

The Defensive Man

Defensive man, after the reconstructed man, is the most sensitive and aware. In fact I discovered that a great many reconstructed men went through what they called a 'defensive period' on their road to enlightenment.

His sensitivity manifests itself in a slightly different way though – the defensive man is the most touchy about himself and his position in society. I don't want to put this type of man down, to point the finger and say, 'Oh, look at this sad case, let's tease him cruelly, let's pull his pants down and laugh', but he often leaves himself wide open for ridicule, which then of course causes him to retreat further into his defensive stance.

He is someone who has been greatly affected by the rise of feminism, who sees women around him as getting more and more powerful, sees himself becoming more and more put upon, and feels uneasy about it. It's not so simple as to say he feels it's time to make a stand and say enough is enough. That is far too like a normal male reaction. The defensive man is, however, constantly looking for ways which prove his deeply held feeling that 'things are just unfair'.

I got a beautiful example of this from Simon Young, a defensive man who was in my study group until he felt that I was putting men down too much. He said:

> It's just not fair, women are always saying I'm sexist. What about them? They can be really really sexist. You know. I mean, what about them. It's just not fair. I'm not sexist. It's all pretty stupid if you ask me. So, if I find women sexy, what am I supposed to do about that. Feel guilty I suppose, whip myself? I'd have thought it was natural, you know, to want to look at a girl's breasts. Flattering even, you know, to mention to a woman that you can make out her nipples through her jumper, you know, with a smile, not leering. But no, it's sexist. Everything's sexist if you ask me. It's not fair.

The defensive man has an obsession with fairness, as though anything in adult life is ever fair. This of course may be a clue, possibly making the assumption yet again that a fully grown male constitutes an adult. Assuming he is capable of adult behaviour could be a serious mistake.

Another favourite defensive male accusation of unfairness made at women is connected with life expectancy. Defensive men like to point out that it is a world-wide phenomenon that women outlive men, that girl children have a better chance of surviving than boys, and that most women will live to appreciate the rewards of their male partners' work for many years after he has passed on.

Defensive Male View of Comparative Life Expectancy

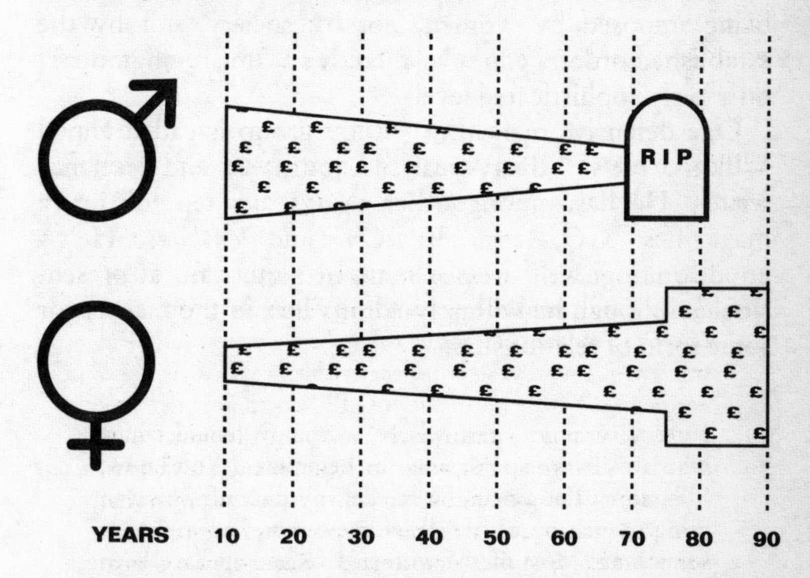

This is an interesting theory, but one that doesn't stand up to a great deal of close scrutiny. For a start, the reasons for greater longevity amongst women are many and various; as usual, no problem is going to have a quick and simple solution.

One reason is certainly to do with stress. Because, since the industrial revolution, men have had to leave the home and spend most of their waking hours struggling in the collective 'marketplace', they have peeled years off their life expectancy. Stress also comes from an inability to express emotions, from internal blocking, which, although at root psychological, has many physical manifestations. Tight shoulders and buttocks being the classic signs amongst the vast majority of adult men, we now know this will also mean tight heart valves, lungs and digestive organs.

However, the defensive man sees this extra stress as being imposed by women, not by society, not by the established order, i.e. not by men. It's blame re-alignment* on a fairly sophisticated level.

One defensive man in my study group is called David Wilkins. He's a thirty-year-old journalist and freelance writer. He has, among other things, written for many magazines – *GQ, Arena, Men Only* and *Penthouse*. He's a good looking, well dressed man, he's quite fit, at present single, although he willingly admits he's in the market for some form of relationship.

> I get very angry, particularly at wimpy feminist men who are always apologising for being men. You know, 'Oh, sorry I'm a man, let me cut my dick off', kind of thing. I mean, as if all women were all right or something! Most of the women I've known have been right cows. Aggressive, assertive, I mean it wasn't them who needed assertiveness training, it was me. I spent far too long feeling apologetic, you know, feeling guilty. Like, about rape, you know, the 'all men are rapists' theory. It's rubbish. I'm not a rapist, I think all women want to be victims, that's far more likely. Most of the

* Blame re-alignment will be explained in detail later.

> women I've known have wanted to be thrown down on the bed and 'had', you know, that's what they've said. Then, before you know it, they're accusing you. Not that this has ever happened to me you understand. But that's my point, they're so manipulative, they'll milk you dry. It's not fair.

It's clear that David has a lot of slightly unfocussed anger to deal with, exclusively aimed at the opposite sex.

The defensive man isn't always that difficult to spot, though there is a confusing area between him and the self-loathing man. I think you could call him the semi reconstructed self-loathing defensive man. I know some women would just prefer to call him an annoying git, but I am trying to be constructive here.

This sort of man appears, on the surface at least, to agree with even the most strident of feminist writers, such as Valerie Solanas' *SCUM manifesto** and Tandy Millet's infamous, *Don't Shit on My Sister! Women Fighting Back!*, published in 1988. This searing indictment of male attitudes caused one defensive man, Roger Wollock, to react in what first appears to be a very non-defensive male way. He said:

> After I read the book, well, what can you say. She's right, all men should be made to read this book. They should be forced to, they should be forced to at gunpoint by women. It's true, men have treated women badly, for centuries, it's true. What can I do? Sure, I'm a rapist, all men are, what can I do about it? Nothing. She's told me everything I don't want to hear about myself and it's all true. Maybe I should campaign for better street lighting so I don't rape the wrong woman

* SCUM standing for the Society for Cutting Up Men.

> on my way home at night! I mean, there's obviously no hope for men according to the book. We're all so evil we may as well, you know, just be pigs. If women hate us that much what's the point. I've got a dick, therefore I am bad. It's so simple. She's right. I can't argue with her.

This is then, the classic defensive male response. The one that feels the accusations, feels the anger and frustration of women, doesn't duck it like the normal man, or try and rationalise it and deal with it maturely like the reconstructed man. He takes it full in the face, and, not unlike a surly adolescent schoolboy trying to resist the discipline of the brutal teacher, 'stands there and takes it'. The arguments are now so overwhelming that only the most insensitive and brutalised male can deny or ignore them. The defensive man cannot, but he also cannot bear the fact that he has to be tarred with the same brush. He's so tired of denying that he's a rapist, he's taken the reactionary, adolescent route of saying '*yes I am a rapist, and I may as well go out and do it.*'

Having said that, he would always backtrack on that when he saw the horror and fear on women's faces, and it is very unlikely that he would commit a sexual assault, but that is not the point.

Unlike the normal man who is an emotional child, the defensive man is emotionally an adolescent boy, prone to sulks, sudden mood changes, crass attempts at deception and passionately held beliefs that are liable to change at a moment's notice. He is confused by his lusts and feels his erection is the most unwanted thing, he feels women hate him for being what he is, but he doesn't hate himself, as does the self-loathing man, and this causes emotional friction.

Of all the men we are looking at, the defensive man is in many ways the most unhappy. He is the one many liberal feminist women will fall in love with in the hope that he will change, or that they can 'change him a bit'. Too classic.

Far be it from me to judge, and certainly it's impossible to generalise, but as an overall view of this type of man and his ability to find his way through the minefield of contemporary sexual politics, without putting too fine a point on it, and not wanting to go on too long with provisos and exceptions, I'd say, generally, that if she believes she can change him, she must have come down with yesterday's rain.

The Self-Loathing Man

This sort of man is at the opposite end of the spectrum to the defensive man. The early seventies 'feminist man' was the precursor of the self-loathing man. This man thrives on guilt, he will be able to express a true and deep-seated hatred for his gender at any time of the day or night. To say he is obsessed is putting it mildly, this sort of man will see all problems as coming from inside,* from his male soul; no matter what the problems are, no matter who may have caused an upset, it is somewhere along the line, his fault. The term used for this sort of man in the pre-sexual-consciousness-raised era would probably have been Vicar.

The self-loathing man will use the term 'as a man' very often, as we can see in this quote from Timothy Wetstone, a self-loathing man who spends a great deal of time in both state-funded and private therapy.

* As opposed to the normal man who sees all problems as coming from outside.

> I just can't help it, if I read of some atrocity in the paper, I always feel implicated. Soldiers killing children or something, I think, I could have done that, I'm no better. I read the papers avidly, maybe I am looking for atrocities, that'd be just about typical, that I, as a man, actually look for horror to feed some sort of oppressed sadistic streak in myself. There's no cure for it other than death or castration. I mean, most men should be given a pill or something, because they're so horrible. But of course there's no research into the whole area of men's aggression, because the whole of society is dominated by men, and patriarchy, and I, as a man, am implicated in that, all the way, up to my male and insensitive neck.

The self-loathing man is also highly competitive with women. No matter what sort of man-hating, ball-breaking, unsympathetic, sadistic women he comes into contact with, he will always strive to outdo her in his criticism of his own gender.

Theories as to why this happens range from plain and simple self-hatred through to wishing to convince the woman that she is right in her conviction that all men are indeed bastards, but that the ones that know they are bastards are slightly less awful than those who don't.

It is thought that some men might use the self-loathing stance as a way of becoming more intimate with very fierce, short haired, feminist women, as this is generally the type of woman the self-loathing man finds attractive.

Graham Turrell was very interesting on this point, he said:

> I met Sandy at a Men Against Sexism meeting in 1979. She was in a group called 'The Fierce as Fuck Wimmin' who did poetry and rapping at women-only events. This

night they had agreed to appear at a mixed event only to make a point that most men would look at the women's work using old patriarchal methods of judgement as to merit and talent. I agreed with this, and for a while stood in the room with my eyes shut and my hands over my ears so I wouldn't judge it along those lines. Eventually my friend Bob told me to watch and stop being such a div. As soon as I saw Sandy, typical for a man I know, but I wanted to have some sort of really, really gentle relationship with her, some sort of non penetrative sexual thing. If she wanted. Of course I assumed she was a lesbian, and I was fully prepared to accept that, and if I discovered she had children, I would have happily looked after them for the rest of my life, in an attempt to make up for the huge shortfall of childcare provision which was due to a massively sexist patriarchal conspiracy which I, as a man, was responsible for. I met Sandy when she had finished doing her gig, and we talked a little bit about pornography, rape and male aggression. It turned out after a long time that she was heterosexual, she just shaved her head for effect; she also said she fancied me. I couldn't believe it, and told her she had been duped by some sort of patriarchal romantic notion of love that was really a screen behind which hid a huge monster of male aggression and violence. She eventually got off with my best friend Bob, and they've been together ever since. It's okay though, I spend a lot of time looking after their kids.

I thought this was a fascinating story, and many people may at first reading consider Graham to be a classic reconstructed man. The big difference here is that Martin has not got in touch with his vanity, his feelings of self-worth are so low that they do not read on any scale we know, as we can see here.

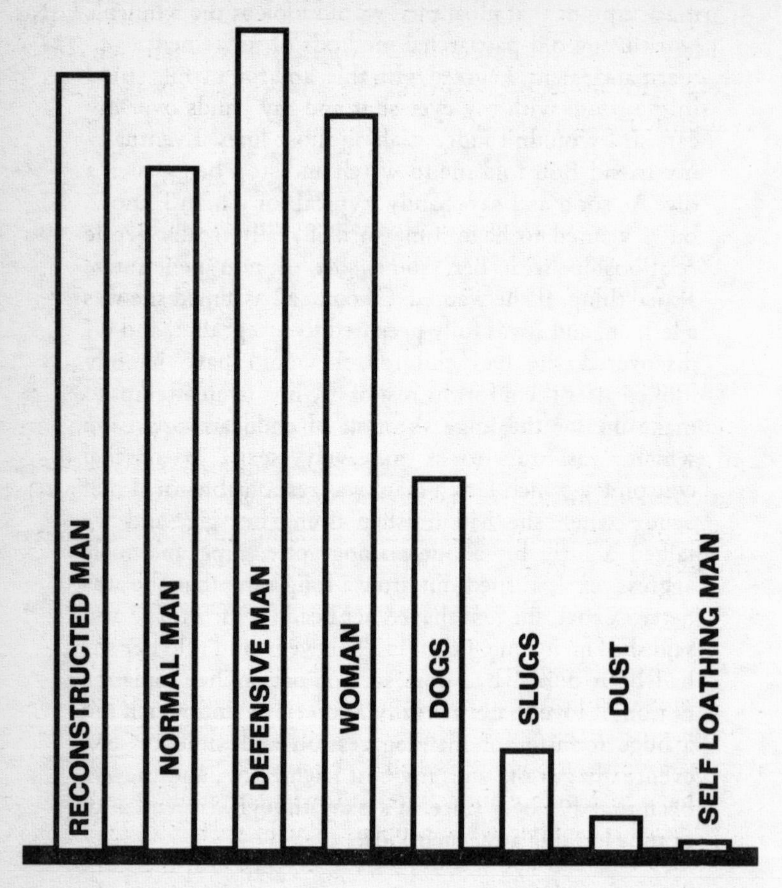

This information was gathered by a series of questionnaires developed at Cambridge University by Professor Terry McNichol, himself something of a self-loathing man. He is however a slightly different type.

Terry is married with two children; his wife had a career

in marketing but has given that up because she felt she dropped out of the world of work when she had the children Terry claimed he wanted but has shown little interest in since their birth. He thinks this is typical of academic men, as he said:

> ... a stupid pathetic desire to prove one's virility by producing offspring. I might have known I'd react like that, I make myself sick.

However, much to the surprise of some people, Terry is what is affectionately known in some male circles as, 'an old shagger'. He is always chasing women, usually young students, although he has made attempts at liaisons with check-out girls, waitresses, shop assistants, in fact virtually any woman he meets.

> ... I can't help it. Well, I probably can, but I don't bother which is what really makes me sick. I'm always having affairs, but as soon as I've slept with the woman. Oh goodness, it's the same every time. I have to rush back to Margaret in a state. I just hate myself. I can't really remember what happens, I'm in such a state, I throw myself about a lot, I bang my head on the wall. We've found a special bit of wall in the kitchen where I don't do too much damage and I don't wake the kids. But I get in such a state, and afterwards, as I'm lying on the floor crawling around begging forgiveness, I swear to myself that I will never do it again. I swear so loud that my voice goes hoarse, but, two months later I'm looking at another 19-year-old fresh-women and it's too late.

As far as I can gather Margaret always used to tell him she really doesn't mind that much.

The last time I spoke to Terry he had just had an affair with an eighteen-year-old Danish undergraduate and Margaret had thrown him and the children out of the house. Terry claimed to be really pleased that Margaret had finally seen that he was a '*complete and utter shit*'.

Terry's therapist, a good friend of mine, told me she thought his incessant desire to sleep with every women he met was something to do with a constant need to hide from the real horror of 'being'. The inability to face the true emptiness and void which we all have to come to terms with at some point during our existence. She claims to confront Terry with this horror every time she has a session with him, and all he tries to do is get off with her.

Interesting Theories on Low Male Fertility Rates

An interesting side-issue which many people would not instantly connect with the self-loathing man has come to light recently. Research in Sweden has shown that the average sperm count in a single Western male ejaculation has dropped by some 50% since 1940. This very worrying trend has obviously caused a great deal of concern to many people, not least the number of men who find it difficult to father a child.

One theory which is gathering strength in psychological

circles is the phenomenon of the 'self-loathing sperm'. It's accepted that sperm carry all the genetic messages of the male, all his physical and psychological traits, wrapped in a microscopic package. If the 'donor' is a self-loathing man, then some of this attitude is going to be inherited by the little white fellow.

Psychologists suggest that as the sperm swims up toward the egg, it gets very depressed and feels it is not worthy of breaking through the egg's wall – such activity is typical of a violent male attitude. It also apparently feels it is certainly not worthy of starting a life, as the life might turn out to be male and therefore worthless, violent, dirty and disgusting.

Even more recent research has come up with a theory that much the same thing is happening with defensive men. Here again the sperm inherits the traits of the donor, but instead of feeling unworthy it feels that the presence of all the other sperm and only one egg is inherently 'unfair'. It apparently feels the hostile secretions inside the woman's body are 'typical' of aggressive women who always want the upper hand.

There has been a fair amount of resistance to these theories within scientific circles,* but judging by many men's response to the ideas, they clearly have some emotional impact.

In fact, very recently Professor Irene Thomas has been working with theoretically infertile self-loathing men, who, as an exercise, try to love themselves and their sperm when they reach a climax. In the three hundred test cases she worked on, one couple conceived a healthy child. The

* 'Unutterable Drivel!' was how a headline in the *Lancet* responded to this research. I think that shows a very blocked emotional attitude amongst some of the older male journalists who work for that periodical.

other men said they felt that their own sperm was just too horrible and messy, and they didn't deserve children anyway as they were so sexist.

chapter 3

The Difference

I want to discuss some basic areas that help define a picture of what a reconstructed man is, and the differences between him and a normal man. As the reconstructed man is such a new phenomenon, it's important to build up a careful picture of what he is in order to avoid the possible pitfalls of tabloid or possibily clichéd journalism.*

Also, due to their exposure to such information, some normal men are competent at pretending they have been through some sort of process of enlightenment.†

To define these subtle differences between reconstructed and normal men, I shall be dealing with six key areas. These are: the apportionment of blame, the sulk, the psycho-focal conceit, testosterone, guilt, and the sensual self image.

* In saying this I have no wish to denigrate the many journalists who on a weekly basis churn out enormous amounts of information on modern socio-sexual manners and mores. It's just that although *The Reconstructed Heart* is in essense a 'pop psychology' book, I am trying to hold on to that elusive creature, the truth.

† See the section on the New Lad.

Blame

To look clearly at the effects of blame, I'd like to start with an interesting quote I recorded during an interview with John Blake, who is an extreme version of a normal man.

John is a low-achieving bank official from Tring. His wife allows him a 'den' in a small attic room that is crammed with a model railway and ham radio equipment.* John has many problems to contend with in the social arena, one of which is his understanding of personal space in public places. He has a rather unfortunate tendency to stand too near people he doesn't know and smile at them.

> I was driving to work one morning, straining over the back to find my sandwich box the wife packs every day. I will admit to being late and I had my foot hard down, but that's the way we tend to drive in my line of work. I'm not showing off but when you've had the experience I have you can control a vehicle at very high speeds in heavily built up areas. Anyway, something went wrong with the car. Must have been the rack and pinion or the steering assembly which is notorious on those models. I've read loads of articles in motoring magazines about them so it's not just me saying that. Other motoring professionals have claimed the same thing. Anyway, somehow the car ploughed into this bus stop and killed some people. Mostly women and kids actually. I stopped, got out and these other people were looking at me. I said, 'Don't look at me, if she'd put the sandwiches where I'd told her this would never have happened!

* I don't want to paint too negative a picture of John, or imply that he is 'the sort of person' who buys pornography, but he did have quite a stupendous collection of soft core girlie magazines stuffed away in various corners where his poor wife was not supposed to find them.

Anyway, it's a stupid place to put a bus stop, you should sue the council.'

It doesn't matter what has happened, it doesn't matter who is involved, you can guarantee that a normal man will believe it's someone else's fault. This activity is called blame re-alignment and is a very common normal male practice.

Blame Re-Alignment in 'Normal Men'

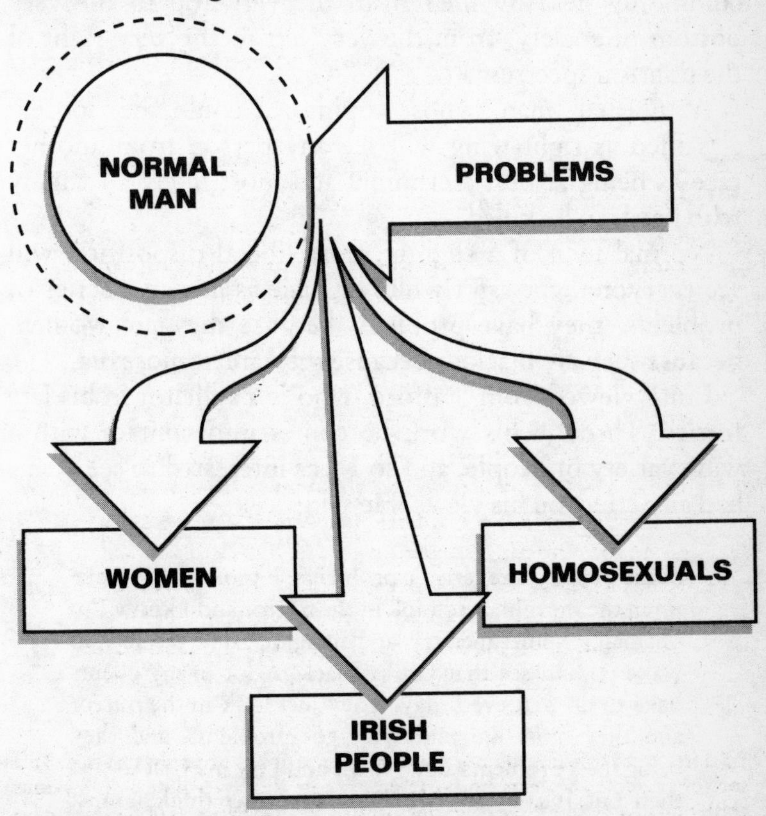

We can clearly see in this diagram the blame coming in from above, instead of being accepted and dealt with internally, is being re-directed towards a group of target areas. Women, homosexuals and Irish people being amongst the most popular.

The normal man sees the rest of the world, outside the white male brotherhood, as a huge mass of incapable people wandering around in a daze. They couldn't do anything if he wasn't there to sort it out. This attitude is commonly held by men from the very top to the very bottom of society, from the very left to the very right of the political spectrum.

A normal man whose opinions could be loosely classified as right wing will see any person from another race as being at best a criminal and most likely an enemy who needs to be killed.

Normal men of a slightly more liberal disposition will see everyone who isn't white or male as having a series of problems; they have problems because they are women, because they are black or because they are homosexual.

I interviewed Tom Stafford, who is a solicitor in his late forties. Through his work he comes into contact with a wide variety of people, and so I was interested to see if this had any effect on his views. He said:

> Some people have terrible problems, I know that. I wake up in the morning and look in the mirror and I know I'm normal. I sometimes try and imagine what it's like to wake up and see that you're black. A lot of my clients have to do that every day. They just look in the mirror and they must know they've got problems, and they bring their problems along to me and I try my best to sort them out. It's the same with women, I often think, it must

> be such a problem waking up every morning to find you're a woman and you've got to deal with all that prejudice. It must be terrible. I'm grateful I'm normal, unlike a lot of men, I don't take it for granted.

As we can see only too clearly, normal men perceive all problems as coming from outside, from other people. They live their lives feeling that the rest of the world, and particularly womankind, is at fault for not 'understanding them'.

The Sulk

Of all the areas I'm dealing with here, the sulk is the most British. I have confronted men from Italy, Turkey, India, Australia, the United States, Canada and France about this activity, and none of them seems to know what I am talking about. They understand shouting, rowing, cat-calling, treating women as sexual objects, using offensive sexist language, dominating the conversation, being bullish, piggish and generally boorish. They can be right on, right off, up themselves, vain, greedy, lazy and downright dangerous. But they don't sulk.

Quite simply, sulking is what British men do for large portions of their lives. They withdraw from the foray, they retreat behind a wall of sullen silence and stay there for long periods of time, the idea being that they 'punish' the person who upset them.*

* One reason I know about sulking is that I myself sulked for 1978. Notice I said *for* 1978, not *in* 1978. I mean I sulked from roughly 3 January when I had a row with my live-in-lover, until 28 December when I started to talk to her again. Bit of a waste of time on reflection.

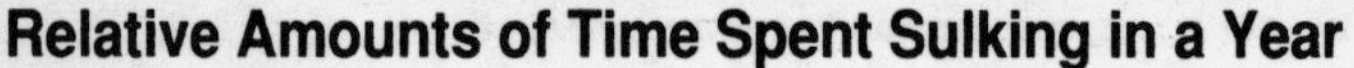

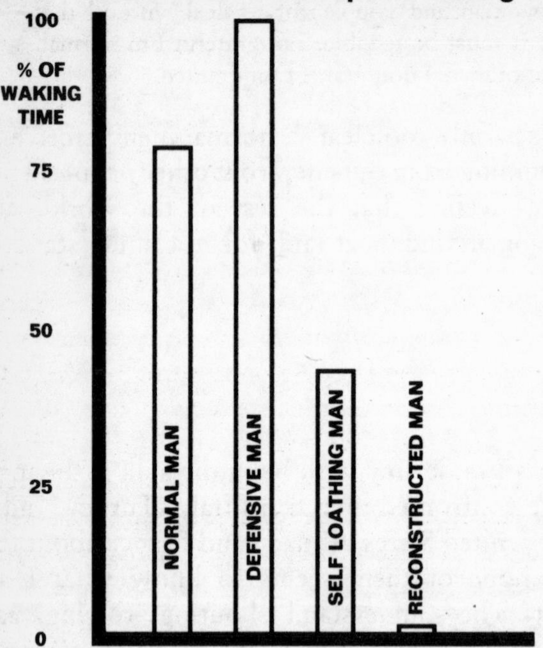

As we can see from this graph, the amounts of time spent sulking can affect a man's life to a very great degree. Indeed a recent survey has discovered that as many working days are lost through male sulking as are lost through the common cold or alcohol abuse.

I asked normal man Barry Tenderton if he ever sulked. This was a bad way of putting the question, I should have been more sensitive because he pouted, folded his arms and looked out of the window. When I leant forward to touch his arm and re-assure him that I was only trying to help, he wriggled away from me and glowered at the ground, making a small whining cross puppy sort of sound. After about an hour of careful coaxing he finally decided to talk.

> It's her fault. She's always going on at me. It's not fair. I just sit in the corner and look at the ground for about a month. That shows her. If she asks me anything, I just don't answer. It's the only way I can get back at her. If I let her get me talking I say all the wrong things and end up looking like a pillock. I can't stand that. So I stay very, very quiet for a long, long time. That really gets on her nerves.

We can see here then that the sulk is a defensive mechanism, used by men when they feel slightly inadequate in the presence of their female partners. It is only unusual in adult men because it is normally used as a bargaining tool by children under the age of five. We all learn as children that if we withdraw our attention, affection and response to an adult, it upsets them brilliantly. We learn that we can really do mummy's head in by not loving her, and then she will buy us the chocolate creme egg at the newsagents.

As we shall see in the next section, this behaviour pattern is generally grown out of by women and the rest of the earth's male population. It seems to be a quaint and touching national quirk that we have developed a race of sulky adult males.

Many professionals in the field have tried to work out why. The defensive male researchers have all naturally blamed the mother, sisters and feminism. The more right on researchers think that British society allows its boys to remain boys as they grow up, and that this lack of development is perpetuated by men and women alike. One theory being bandied around is that many women prefer their men simple and sulky as they are easier to manipulate and control, also a childish man is easier to sell to, to convince to vote for you, and to die for you in the event of a war. It could be argued that keeping the man an emotional child is very much to the benefit of any controlling authority, but this is getting into a pretty macro political area and one I'm not dealing with here.*

The Psycho-Focal Conceit

Research done in the 1920s in the United States showed us how all human beings start out in life with the same basic psychological assumption. We are born 'knowing' that we alone are at the very centre of the universe. Everything in the heavens and earth surrounds us, we are the most important thing there is. Everyone we meet is there for our sole use, they all serve a purpose, to feed us, educate us, move us, clean us, love us. This mental and emotional state is called a Psycho-Focal Conceit, a PFC and it manifests itself in total unremitting selfishness.†

In very small children this is essential to their survival, they have to be dependent on their parents, therefore they must be able to demand without guilt. This state normally disappears as the person matures. As the child grows it will slowly see other children being cared for, and the connections are made. Maybe not *the* centre, but one of

* Classic get-out of course. Just as I start to touch on a more serious political issue, I make an excuse and back away. I suppose that means that I really can't handle the more adult political arguments that face our society. I don't want to talk about it. Shut up and leave me alone. That's it. I'm not going to say another word.

† The term was coined by Professor Hutchins Harrison of the New York Institute of Mental Science. He published a paper in 1921 called, 'The Psycho-Focal Conceit and its Effect on Diagnosis'. It's very boring which is why I didn't quote from it.

The Difference

many centres is a mental state held by many four- and five-year olds. It was discovered that in female children the assumption was no longer held by the time the child had reached the age of six or seven. In males however there were often cases of full blown PFCs in men of forty and fifty years of age.

Levels of Psycho Focal Conceit in Adults

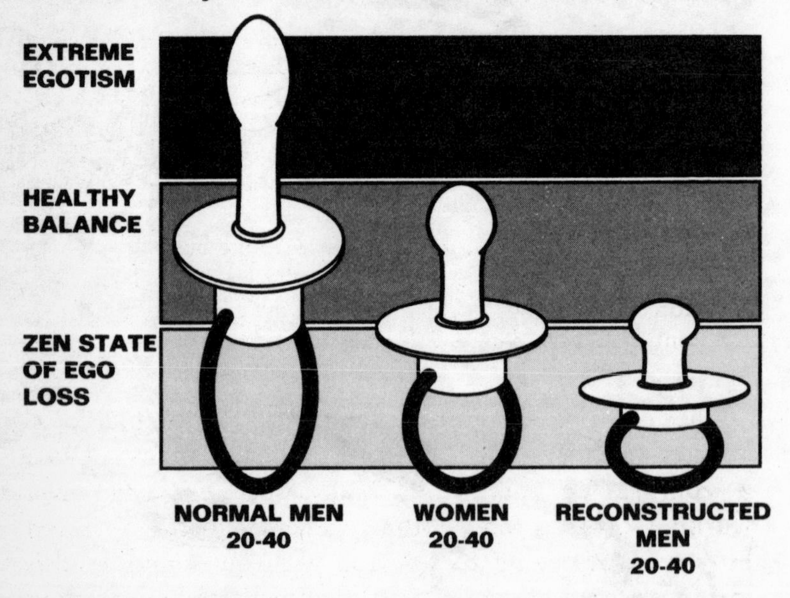

As we can see here, reconstructed men achieve a very favourable reading, they are approaching a zen state of ego loss.* These results have been disputed and the argument continues. One of the factors in the dispute is the

* This is only achieved through intensive psycho-analysis and no attempt should be made by normal men at achieving this kind of reading without full professional support.

reconstructed man's alleged ability to emotionally manipulate the investigators working for the research departments.

We can also see women achieve a healthy balance, and normal men achieve a reading for which a psychological term has not yet been devised.

As an example of these attitudes, the following interview with Nick Frazer, a thirty-nine-year-old water treatment specialist shines some light on the whole issue. Nick was discussing the difficulties he was having with his wife. He claimed to find her unreasonable and demanding.

> She came home soaking wet and asked why I didn't pick her up. Moaned on and on about how long she'd been waiting. I told her I forgot but that wasn't good enough for her. I said moan moan moan as a joke but she just stood there dripping. Of course she had completely forgotten I couldn't take the car out in heavy rain as I'd only just washed it.

The often held assumption amongst the middle or 'chattering'* classes is that this sort of selfishness in a man is confined to the lower, blue collar *nouveau riche*, working classes and other general plebeian types. However, according to research with quiet middle class men with good haircuts, clean fingernails and a reassuring tone of voice, over 72% interviewed suffered from one form of PFC or another.

The reasons behind such a high PFC reading amongst

* The term 'chattering classes' was first used in a *Daily Mail* article to describe what were once called, 'the concerned middle classes'. It is presumably a put-down, although as anyone who has met one will tell you, no one chatters more than a *Daily Mail* journalist.

mature normal males is of course a matter of hotly contested speculation. Some schools of thought have it that due to the mother love that is poured into boy children at an early age, men decide they are on to a good thing and never make the necessary steps toward maturity, remaining emotional five-year-olds all their lives. The confusion this causes is complex, some people making the mistake that a mature man with the emotions of a toddler is going to be in some way stupid. This is clearly not the case, as a trip around any scientific establishment will quickly show. Some of the most brilliant minds in the country are seated in bodies which still suck their thumb at the age of fifty.

Other schools believe that the absent father is to blame, the young boy grows up without any form of mature role model to base his behaviour on. By absent father I am not even talking about children brought up in single-parent families, although I obviously include these. I am referring to boys whose fathers are trapped in the archaic industrial revolution system of being removed to the workplace for huge sections of their waking life, and considering this to be normal. They see their children for an average of three hours a week, and one morning at the weekend.

Nigel Bennet was revealing in an interview I conducted with him on this subject.

> My dad worked for the civil service, I think. I only saw him once or twice a week. He'd rush into the bedroom just as we were going to bed and be all pally. We always liked to see him but wondered who he was. We guessed he was mum's brother or something. At weekends we were supposed to see him but he was always out playing golf. On Sundays he said he got really depressed so he went out.

It is little wonder then, especially considering that their fathers are emotional children, that little boys grow up to be little boys trapped in big men's bodies.*

Testosterone

Testosterone was first discovered in 1908 by Professor Bernard Hielaman who worked for an International chemical company in Basle, Switzerland. Since then, terms like 'testy' and 'tetchy' have come into common usage to describe men who punch holes through walls when they don't get their own way. The concept of the barely controllable man supports the traditional folk myth that men are violent due to their hormones not, as many liberals believe, because of attitudes fostered in them by a patriarchal society, a hostile urban environment and an early exposure to He Man and She Ra® animated cartoons on TV.†

* I have noticed, interestingly enough, that some women find the notion of the little boy in the man's body a highly stimulating erotic image. One women I spoke to went on and on about how her lover was a little boy, and therefore easily emotionally manipulated, but he was inside a big man's body. She made much of the word big, and I only mention it because I suppose she was implying something there. I don't know what.

† Many boys' earliest role is the absurd sized figure of He Man, whose semi-naked form is indestructible. There have been many cases of five-year-old boys challenging thirty-ton trucks armed only with a stick. Psychologists disagree heatedly over the influence of such cultural icons. I myself was greatly influenced by a character called Captain Hurricane who appeared regularly in the Valiant comic book. He spent his time 'smashing' whole Panzer tank divisions with his bare hands. His 'pint sized batman, Maggot Malone' would always warn the reader of impending action with the immortal phrase, 'Uh oh, I think the Cap'n's going to have one of his ragin' furies.'

Testosterone is still used as an excuse for aggressive or anti-social behaviour practised by men. These excuses are used for many types of violent activity from minor football hooliganism through to major international conflict. Controlling its effects has been a major pre-occupation of western society since the dawn of recorded history.

Armies, organised religion and rough and tumble contact sport are all designed to accommodate testosterone without causing too much damage to the surrounding environment. Mickey,* a man I interviewed in a high security correctional facility told me this:

> I went bald very young so I got a taste for punching blokes who had all their own hair. I was in and out of the nick for years. I'd go to a pub, bloke looks at me with all this hair on his head and wallop, down he goes and I'm back inside. They send me to see the doctor about it and he said it was my testosterone levels. I nutted the bastard, I said to him, are you telling me I'm bent or what? He says that all men have this stuff and it's all natural and that. Now when I get arrested I just tell the Bill that I can't help it 'cos of me testosterone and I only have to come and see you.

In the late seventies it was discovered at the Boston Centre for Hormonal Studies that the levels of testosterone vary very slightly during a man's natural monthly cycle. Most men are completely unaware of this taking place but the newly sensitive so-called 'non-sexist men' of the mid to late seventies claimed to have a bit of advantage.

This new consciousness came about after an article on

* Mickey is obviously not this individual's real name. I had to use a false one as he is a dangerous psychotic criminal and he knows where I live.

the subject appeared on the *Guardian* woman's page in September 1978. As we can see, after that date there was a remarkable increase in the perceived levels of testosterone present in the system. It's important to remember these are the *perceived* levels, not the *actual* ones. There was, medically, such a small amount of change it is thought to be impossible to detect.

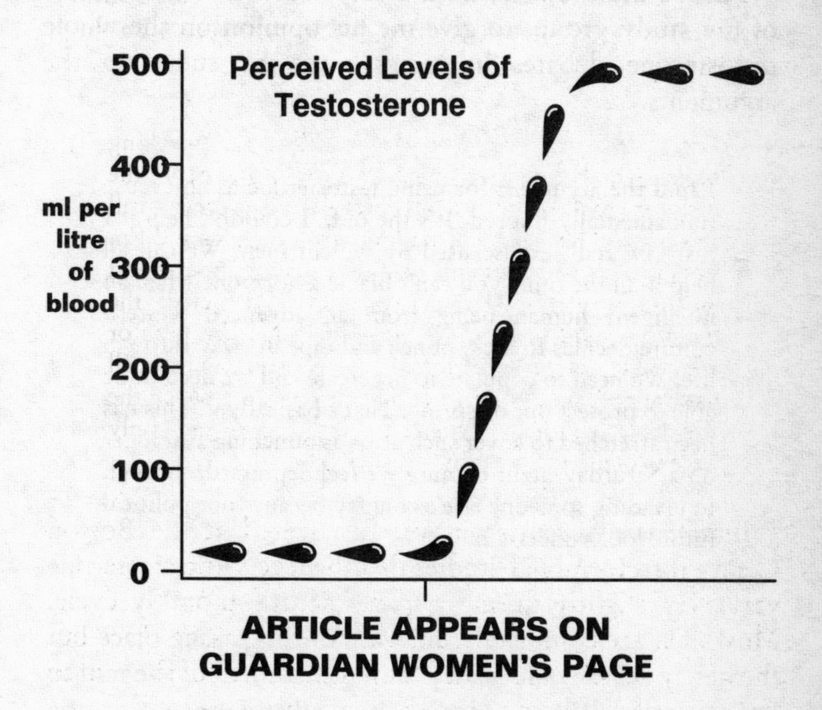

This awareness amongst the tiny 'non-sexist' population manifested itself in many different ways. Some men claimed they would feel more irritable, more horny or more boring at certain times of the month. One or two discovered that occasionally they were not able to do the washing up or hoovering, and general tidying chores could result in long term depressions. Interestingly, the vast majority claimed they felt they needed to indulge in sex with many different women every now and then to help 'balance out' their testosterone levels and that their long-term partners should try and accept this.

I asked Matthew Carlton, a very reconstructed member of my study group, to give me his opinion on the whole testosterone debate. In many ways he sums up the arguments.

> I find the argument for using testosterone as an excuse fundamentally floored. It's the old, 'I couldn't help it I just saw red', excuse used by violent men. We can all help it all the time, you can't blame a hormone when an intelligent human being from an advanced western culture decides to kick, punch and rape his way through life. We need to copulate to procreate and we need to be able to protect our offspring. That's basically it. This has been stretched to cover such areas as punching a stranger on a Saturday night because we feel depressed, through to invading someone else's country because our political future looks uncertain.

Guilt

Guilt as a phenomenon of all classes was only introduced on a popular level after the Second World War. It became common currency in international affairs, and as the forties slowly progressed, seeped its way into people's private lives. The post-war period initially afflicted more right-wing men with guilt. Left-wing hard liners had a guilt-free 'we told you so' period which lasted until the demise of Stalin.

After the revelations of the Gulags, many left-wing men experienced secondary guilt at a pretty devastating level. They didn't let it destroy their dream however, and women were still expected to make the tea and sandwiches at Communist Party gatherings up until the late seventies.

There was talk within the post-war Labour Party of introducing guilt as a compulsory subject for all children over thirteen, but this was later abandoned. There was, however, a Chair of Guilt Studies created at Leicester Polytechnic in 1959, but it was never filled after 1964. The first incumbent, Professor Douglas Johnson, was in fact the only man we know of officially to have died of guilt. It seemed that he lived an utterly blameless life, he loved his wife and children, became a vegetarian and was a tireless charity worker. His last words were, 'I'm so sorry I'm taking so long to die.'

This graph* was developed by Professor Johnson and his team over a twenty-year period. Unfortunately, Professor

* Professor Johnson's team collected samples of guilt levels from all over the UK and have massed the data on one mainframe. Measuring guilt is a very specific skill, and the science connected with it is, as stated by a critic of Professor Johnson's, 'at about the same level of development as television would have been in 1910'.

Johnson felt that publishing the data would be far too judgemental. There were terrible rows within the team, some people didn't speak to each other for years after. It was finally agreed by default to leave the graph blank.

Guilt Levels in Men 1970-1990

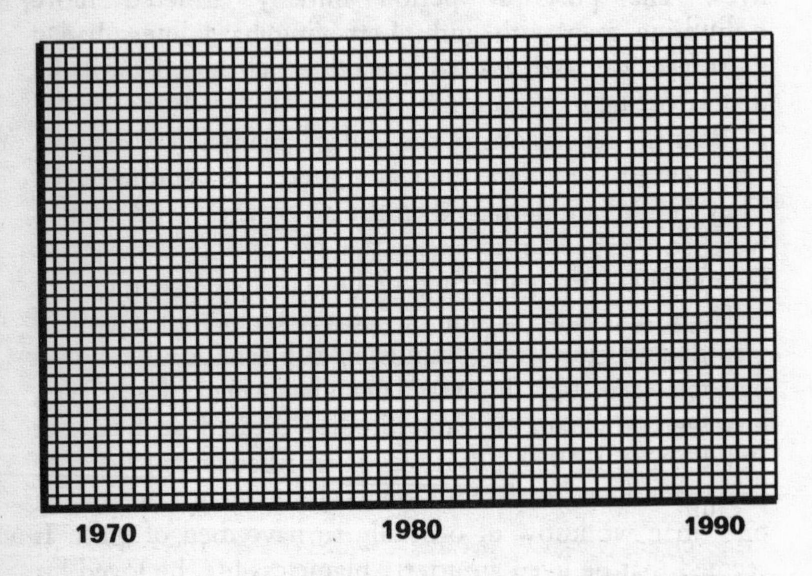

Guilt has to be used very carefully though; it can be an emotional anchor which ties an individual to a certain behaviour pattern for many years. Tom Stafford, a rather sad member of my study group, told me this.

> I'd been married for twenty-odd years before I met Alice. She was the same age as my eldest son, but very pretty. After we had sex the first time I was absolutely racked with guilt. I still love my wife very much but Alice made me feel young again. Soon I only had to

> think about Alice and I would feel guilty, but also very sexually aroused. After three or four months I realised it was the guilt, not Alice that made me aroused. When my wife left me and I moved in with Alice the whole thing fell apart, I didn't feel guilty any more, I haven't had sex now for eleven years, I hope I begin to feel guilty about *that* soon.

Guilt is, however, one of the prime elements in the make-up of a reconstructed man. It was the key to the door that I had been looking for. I wrote in my notes in July 1988,

> Feeling incredibly horny, and guilty. That woman at the party last night who looked like Jodie Foster. I've thought of nothing else all night. Why can't I just think of her as another human being, why do I always see her in a steamy dripping sexual context? I feel so bad. What is it? Guilt. It must be. Guilt is the key. I know I am on this earth to find the answer, that is my calling. Look for the clinical removal of guilt and you have found the reconstructed man.*

Guilt is an interesting emotion, and it is true, it was the first clear way I found towards the discovery of reconstructed behaviour. As we shall see later, the clinical removal of guilt through intensive psychotherapy has resulted in a whole new character. Guilt is a natural emotion found in all human beings from all races, but the reconstructed man has managed to remove it from his emotional vocabulary so to speak.

* I hope people appreciate how deeply embarrassing it is to include this extract from my personal diary. It's always embarrassing, it reveals possible inner levels of self-importance which don't fit with one's public image. However this book does follow a personal journey so I feel I have no choice.

Traditionally, clinical psychologists have known that a man who feels no guilt is likely to be a psychotic murderer. The lack of guilt in a reconstructed man is very different – it's a lack of guilt built on a detailed understanding of his position in the world and his responsibilities therein. Donald Wallace, an architect in his early forties explains:

> The whole guilt thing held me back for years. Now I understand guilt completely. I see it as a negative currency. For instance, if I have an affair with another woman I invest heavily in guilt. If I tell my wife about the affair all I'm doing is off loading that guilt onto her. I see this as very unfair, so I don't tell her.

This new attitude to guilt has set the reconstructed man apart. It is not a denial of guilt, nothing is swept under the carpet. Guilt is rationalised, analysed and finally compartmentalised where it is stored safely until death.

As the reconstructed man is a new phenomenon, we don't actually know what happens to all the stored guilt. We know it has a half-life of at least twenty-five years, but beyond that is mere conjecture.

This rather graphic representation is a projection of what scientists believe might happen over a twenty-year period. It was done using a large graphic-generating computer based in Idaho. Using data developed by NASA based on facial degeneration, a programme was run to show how the human face might be altered over a twenty-year period with no guilt outlet.*

* This research was funded by an obscure arm of the Roman Catholic Church and was designed to prove the theraputic effect of the confessional. Unfortunately when the same tests were run on people who regularly attended mass and confessed their sins to a priest, the degeneration happened at exactly the same rate. The results of the tests were suppressed, and the scientist who carried them out was later found hanging by the neck from Blackfriars Bridge.

Effect of Long Term Guilt Storage

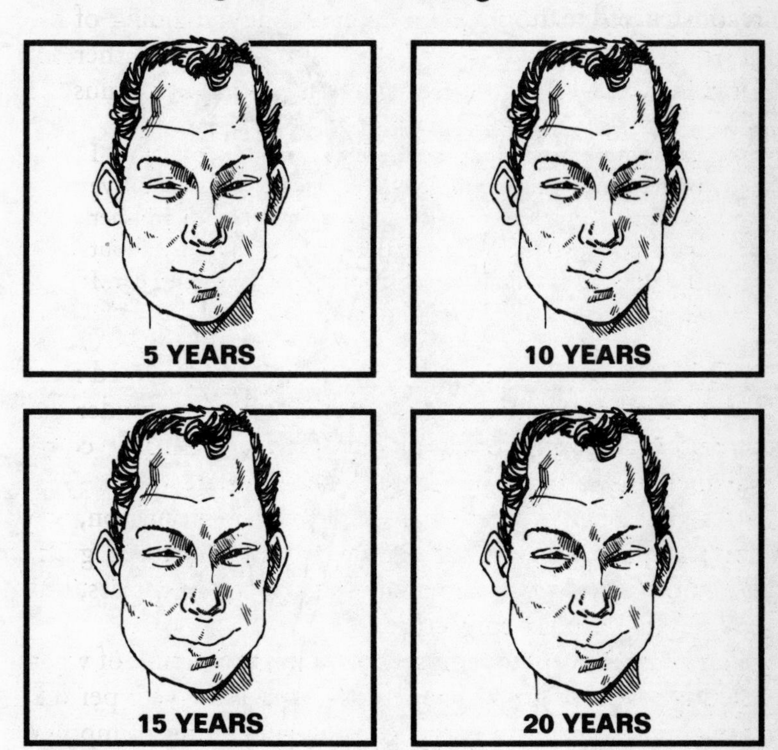

The Sensual Self Image

The sensual self image is something we all carry inside us and is a fascinating area to explore. Research done in Denmark has revealed that the picture created by the way we 'feel' ourselves, through our nerve-endings, our sensuality if you like, is fairly different from the way in which we see ourselves and each other, visually. Nothing better highlights the differences between a normal and reconstructed man.

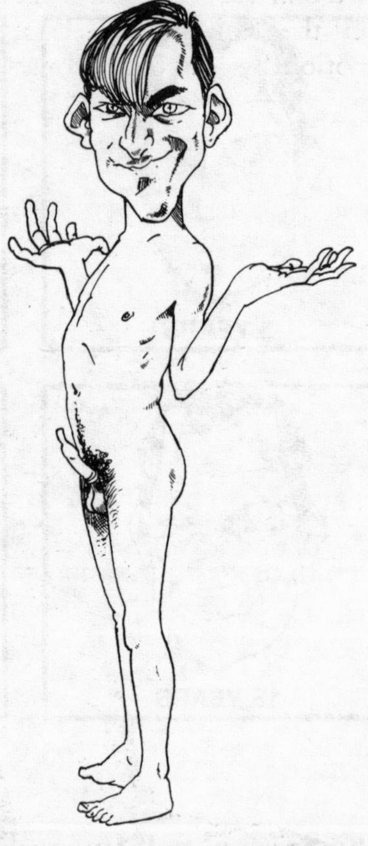

As we can see, in the reconstructed man, the sensual self image is of a non-threatening open and clean body. Large eyes and ears to take in what the woman has to say, long sensitive fingers and a perpetually erect penis already fitted with a condom.

Whereas here we can see the normal man's sensual self image is a little different.

The massive lips and mouth to eat, drink and perform lewd oral acts, the giant grabbing hands to grab I suppose, and the 'roll of carpet' style penis all point to an emotionally undeveloped sense of self.

chapter 4

Reconstruction 1970–90

As the 1970s dawned, a whole new generation of men were waking up from the slumber of two thousand years of patriarchy. Waking up to realise that just possibly men hadn't always been right about absolutely everything.

The feminist movement has been thoroughly recorded and chewed over many times, but the male response to this movement is a less well documented phenomenon. Men in the seventies went through a great many changes. Apart from length of hair and the first tentative challenges to macho stereotypes, many individuals went through a period of intense and high-impact soul-searching. Much was written and spoken during these years, but perhaps the poetry of the period sums up the mood. Here is an example:

> Hear my heart,
> It beats the same as yours,
> Though my body is hard,
> My feelings are soft.
> I am no warrior,
> I return only from toil.
> I need care as much as you need it.
> I'm quite nice.*

* I wrote that myself at the age of twenty-one and gave it to a young woman I was courting. I had failed to notice she was a committed lesbian separatist.

The response from the women's movement was fairly hostile. It was as if men thought they could do a bit of washing up, learn to cry and write a poem and the sins and torment of five thousand years of patriarchal oppression would be washed away in a moment.

As time has progressed this has proved to be a dangerous myth. Many undeveloped theories have been bandied about in an attempt to justify the continued need for a man to be perpetually serviced by women. Under different guises and excuses, men often still manage to move from the protection and nurture of a mother to the constant attention of a woman lover or wife with little or no upset.

The breakdown of the system of marriage might be seen to stem from this clash of needs. Women no longer being satisfied and men being overwhelmingly satisfied with exactly the same situation is bound to lead to certain stresses within any relationship and on a larger scale within society. However, it is not fair to tar all men with the same brush and some more radical male groupings attempted to challenge these traditions in the seventies.

Men's Groups

Men's groups were fairly formalised groupings that flowered from mid-August 1971 until about 12 July 1982. The arrival of the Thatcher government here (and Reagan in America) and consequent cultural upheaval put paid to any form of soul-searching, and as anyone in marketing will tell you, men's groups were not seen as a particularly exciting fiscal growth area.

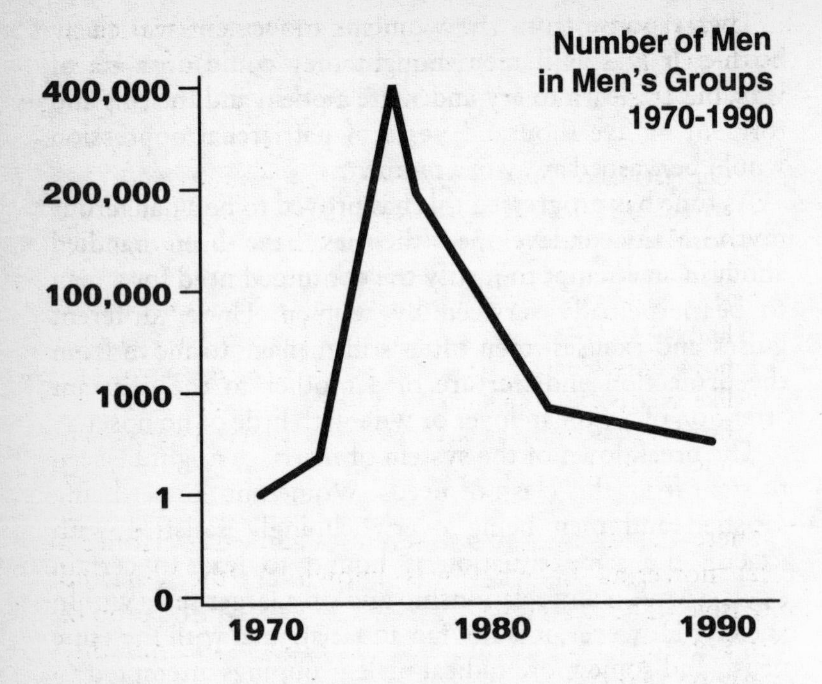

As we can see from this graph, in the late seventies, upwards of 400,000 men joined men's groups for a very limited period. In late June 1988, one man, Geoffrey Vickers, was still going to a men's group on his own, above a bookshop in Peterborough.

Although they were organised along non-hierarchical lines, there was always someone called a 'facilitator' to help 'guide' the group. This was a notion directly imported from women's consciousness-raising groups which flowered in the sixties. The facilitator merely helped the whole group steer themselves in the way they wanted to go. To find out more I interviewed Doug Phillips. When he was attending a men's group he worked in an adventure playground in a deprived inner city area. He now operates his own design consultancy company from Greenwich in south-east London. His reminiscences went on for many days, but this particular incident stood out:

> Our facilitator made everyone feel guilty when they arrived by looking at his watch and then assuring them it was fine and there was no rush. Someone had to massage his shoulders all the way through the session – he claimed that his acupuncturist told him facilitating made him tense. He'd shout right in your face and tell you how sexist you were, he said he needed to be aggressive like that because sexism was so deeply ingrained into men that it needed a harsh shock to 'rip it out and stomp it to a pulp'.

There was during the late seventies and early eighties a brief flowering of what was known as 'the weekend intensive'. This would be organised by a loose affiliation of men's groups that communicated through the monthly magazine *Spare Part*.*

The weekend intensive men's group was a very specific event and there was always a range of 'workshops' to attend. The titles of the workshops give some idea as to the nature of the activities which took place. For example at a weekend intensive held in Totnes in Devon in 1981 you could go to workshops on the following:

> 10 am – 12 noon
> I feel guilty, therefore I am.

* *Spare Part* was seen as an answer to the feminist magazine, *Spare Rib*. The editors, Steve and Nigel, were very keen to point out that this was not meant to be the idea. They said they got very depressed by that sort of accusation, they felt it was divisive and typical of the way men get at each other in a competitive patriarchal environment.

spare part

55p (sorry)

a magazine for men

(that women can buy as well) (but don't have to)

Roger Pillock on being miserable

Sex and guilt, the great combination

Wanking, should we stop?

The C word: The debate continues

Enter our competition: How right on are you?

plus all the latest reports from men's groups around the country

1 pm – 3 pm
Living with the Biological Chain of Events that I call me.

5 pm – 7 pm
From Volvo to Vulva. Learning to Understand Women.

Whatever we may think of them now, these sessions were not an easy cop-out. The men involved took them very seriously, they spent thousands of hours sitting in overheated empty schoolrooms with no shoes on, trying to work out what to do. A whole generation of men, it seemed, were weeping away the best years of their lives, as if they were paying for the sins of their forefathers. This weeping was being done at the weekends, at a time when 'normal' men were out playing golf, visiting prostitutes or getting involved in drunken football-related violence. No one needed to go to a weekend intensive, they did it of their own free will. Mostly they were uplifting and regenerative experiences, but as Jack Williams, a facilitator of long and grinding experience remembers, things sometimes went very wrong indeed:

> We were doing a very good workship on homophobia, I had a couple of men in my group crying hysterically and I was pleased it was going so well. Then the door burst open and Terry ran in the room. He was going through some very powerful emotions and expressing them freely. He said, 'Please, come quick, Nick is trying to cut his penis off, I think he needs the support of a group, I can't cope.' We all got up and went to the door. We looked into the hall and there was this man who I didn't know, he was naked and trying in vain to cut off his penis with a pair of child's plastic paper-cutting scissors. It was just one of those things you had to deal with.

The Role of the Individual Analyst

Towards the end of the eighties and the development of an individualist free market culture, more and more men turned to engaging an individual analyst to help them develop as individuals or sort out the terrible mess they were in. No longer did men sit around in groups with no shoes on learning how to cry, they sat in beautiful rooms with one qualified professional who guided them towards their destiny.

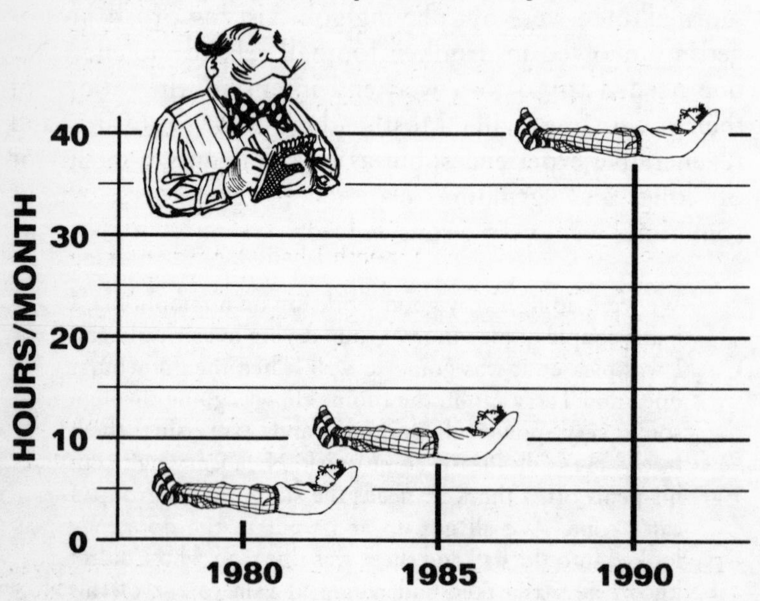

This graph, put together by the Institute for the Study of

Depression* shows how during the eighties more men spent more and more time in long-term, in-depth consultation with their analyst.

Over the weeks and months of often very expensive analysis, men would attempt to shed five thousand years of patriarchal guilt. They would approach concepts such as 'responsibility without guilt', 'love without guilt' and at the highest level, 'lust without guilt'.

I asked study group member Peter Bradshaw about his experiences with his therapist, and why he went in the first place.

> In the early eighties I was generally very pissed or ripped out of my skull in one way or another. I chain smoked all day, chain drank all night and at weekends I was generally doing some pretty heavy drug abuse. With the help of ex-lovers I started doing analysis. Well, if I'm honest what I mean is, when women packed their bags and stormed out of my life, they would usually shout out something like, 'You're mad, you're a weirdo, you need to see someone!', just before they slammed the door. So I did. Within a month I had stopped smoking and drinking, I started riding a push bike and eating organic food. I'm still bored out of my mind but I feel better physically.

As we can see from Peter's testimony, it was generally during these periods that clients found they spontaneously started to give things up in a big way.

* The Institute for the Study of Depression is based at Manchester University in a rather grimy shed at the rear of a nondescript building off the Oxford Road. The windows look out on to a burnt-out youth project which has a defaced mural on one wall depicting people of many races joining happily together in an idyllic urban landscape. When I visited in June 1990, the place was deserted but I found large quantities of data scattered about which made sobering reading.

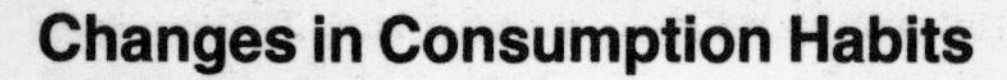

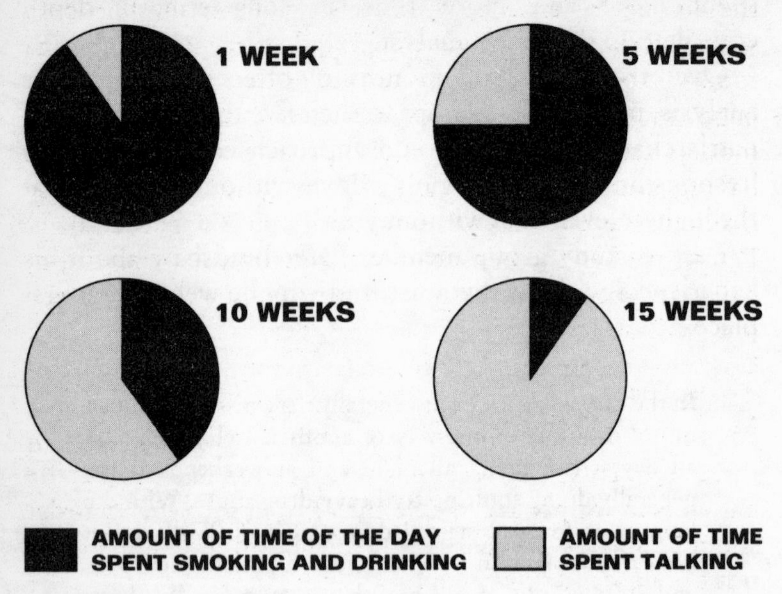

This graph shows us that there does seem to be a very strong connection between the constant decrease in the amount of alcohol and tobacco used, and the constant increase in the amount of time men found they needed to talk about deeply disturbing personal problems in public. No firm psycho-sexual formulation has come out of this data as yet, but there are many theories.

Women have commented that they don't see why they have to suddenly listen to men talk about their emotions for hours once these men realise they have them. It seems that many proto-reconstructed men start to let it all out in a major way once they have broken through their emotional blocks.

I asked Peter Bradshaw if he'd noticed any difference in the amount of time he spent talking. Peter used to be a social worker, but during his period of reconstruction he found he was talking to his clients far too much and they began to complain about him. On one occasion a single mother came in to see him about the problems she was having with her ex-boyfriend: she wasn't getting any maintenance, the bills were mounting up, she needed help. Peter gave her the benefit of his theories for three-and-a-half hours before she burst into tears and had to be helped out. He had to change careers and is now studying to be a child psychologist and professional nanny.

I have had to edit Peter's quote quite rigourously. In answer to one question he was able to fill both sides of three separate C180 cassette tapes. He even had some spare batteries in his pocket in case the ones in my tape recorder should run out. I eventually managed to ask him if he'd noticed he was talking more. He said:

> Yes, I talk much more, I don't know what it is, but I just need to tell people, particularly women, how complicated all my emotions are. It's amazing, I'm amazing, we're all amazing, and even though that sounds like a hippyish thing to say, it has to be seen in the context of a far more advanced and amazing series of thought processes. I mean, talking is communication isn't it, in some ways. I mean, I love talking now, I really love it. I can sit and talk for hours, I often do. I went to Glastonbury in '89, but I didn't see any bands, I just sat in a tent for the whole weekend and talked. I talked all day and all night, finding new areas of my heart, my emotions, or whatever you want to call them, all overflowing with things, different feelings and fears and thoughts and ideas. It was great, really really great. I

> went to a party once, it was great, one of those really, really great parties, there was loads of people there, and instead of dancing and getting drunk, we all stood around and talked, for ages. It was great. There's something about me though, because at the end I was still there, talking. Everyone else had gone home or gone to bed I suppose, but I was still having a great time. After the party I left and went to a greasy spoon café and I talked in there for a few hours before going to bed. Marathon talking I suppose. Is that enough or d'you want me to say anything else? I mean, I could go on if you liked.

If a woman can't bear the prospect of this non stop psycho-babble, she will find he will listen to her after he's heard on a radio programme, or read in a newspaper, that men never listen to women. If she can surreptitiously arrange for this information to fall in his path, she will have a willing ear for three or four hours until something she says sparks off a string of theories of his own.

Reconstruction Through Therapy

So, how exactly does the process of reconstruction take place? Through careful counselling, whispered suggestion and hint-dropping, an analyst will attempt to encourage and nurture the positive aspects of a man's heart, the negative aspects will be dissected and removed.

Some emotions, such as unprovoked aggression and guilt, will be 'withdrawn' from use, while others, such as transcendental patience are completely fabricated. No natural responses occur, no action takes place without careful thought. As in the analogy of the old house, some walls have been knocked down to make the internal space feel more open. Consequently, new walls have been built in order to stop the whole structure collapsing.

For so long, men were blocked, unable to describe their feelings. Through analysis men learned a whole new language, their feelings were peeled open and laid bare for inspection. The assumption among many people is that if someone undertook such a difficult journey of recovery and self-discovery, they might lose a great deal of self-confidence. This has been proved to be absolutely not the case.

Doctors Peter Tidwell and Cranforth O'Donahugh of the Sydney Institute of Humanitarian Sciences* have devised a system of measuring the levels of self-confidence in a person using heart rate, blood pressure, pupil dilation, blood sugar levels, palm sweatiness and anal tightening. They attached monitoring devices on two men and recorded levels over an average working day. The first man, Jack Davies, was defined as 'normal'. He worked in the accounts department of David Jones, a large Australian department store chain. At the end of the test day he was asked to describe what had taken place during the day. His anecdotes were then tied in with various readings. This graph shows how he held up during his average day at home and at the office.

* S.I.H.S. was set up as an inaugural research and development wing of Sydney University in 1982. It was funded by a tax free gift from Dave Fitzgibbon, a publicity shy oil and newspaper multi-billionaire who suffered terribly from lack of self confidence.

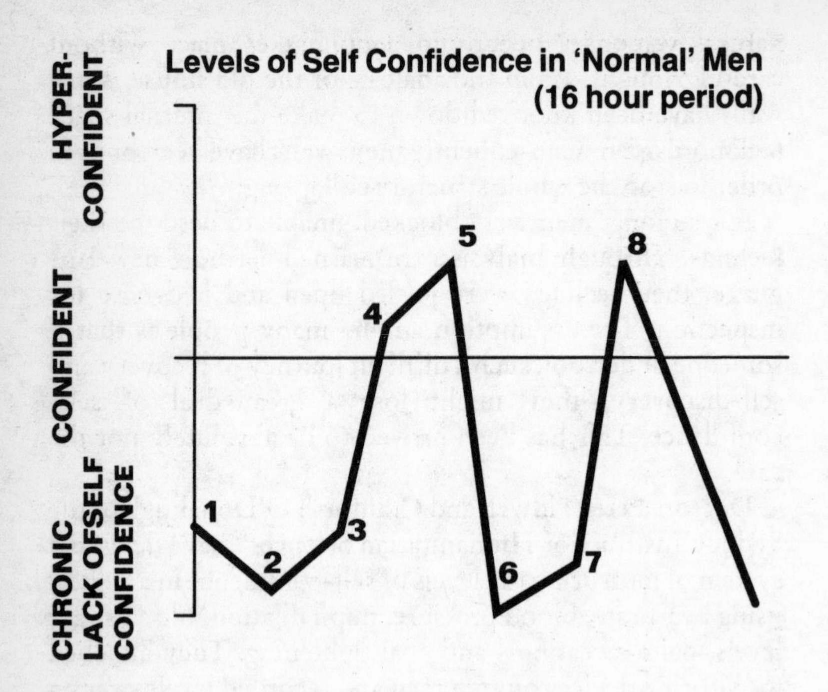

1 At the start of his day he woke up and looked in the mirror, an experience which he felt lowered his confidence level.

2 He then blamed his wife for everything which lifted him up a little.

3 Here he managed to aggressively push into a traffic jam on his way to work, this made him feel a good deal better, he described in detail the pleasure he got from looking at 'the sucker' behind him fuming at the wheel.

4 At this point it appears he claimed to have had an original idea at work to do with keeping tabs on despatch items. He was congratulated for this by his superior.

5 However, unfortunately for Jack, his secretary managed to prove the idea was in fact hers, and he was severely reprimanded.
6 He arrived home and blamed his wife for everything
7 before going to the pub and telling everyone how well he's doing at work.
8 And obviously this is where he returned home, attempted sexual intercourse, failed, and blamed his wife.

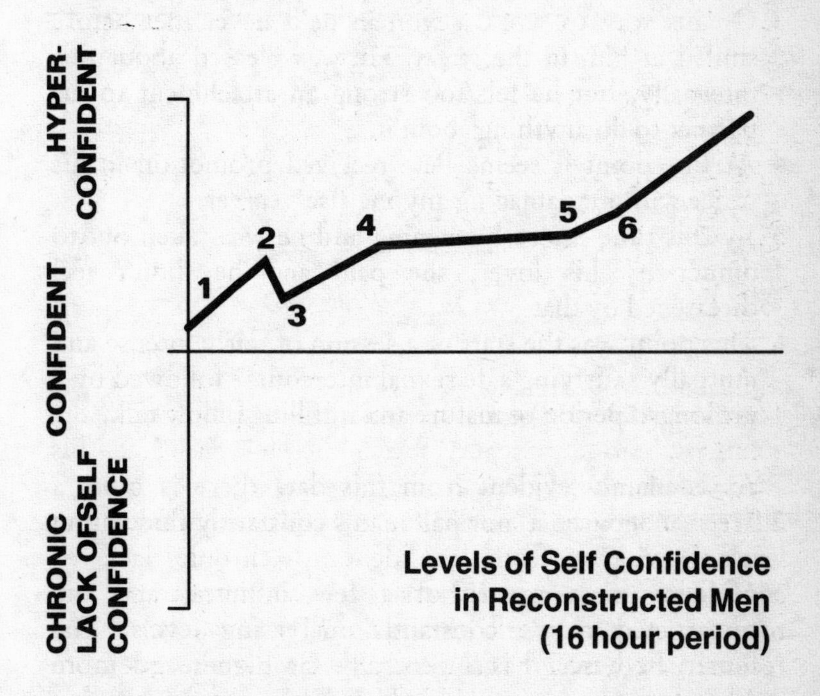

In contrast, in this graph, we can see a very different picture emerging. This was recorded using exactly the same system, only this time the device was attached to Pete Dickerson, a thirty-year-old graphic designer who works at a practice which is housed in a neat converted warehouse property on the Rocks area of Sydney.

1 At this point Pete woke up already feeling confident because his dreams had all been conducted within a positive dream framework he had devised with his therapist.
2 He later read about male violence in the *Sydney Morning Herald* and felt in some way implicated.
3 On his way to work a woman he'd never met before smiled at him in the street. He was pleased about this internally, but he felt too strong an attachment to his partner to do anything about it.
4 At this point it seems Pete received promotion in his office without damaging anyone else's career.
5 By this time it's early evening and he was taken out to dinner by his lover, she paid and he didn't feel threatened by that.
6 This point was the start of a session of fairly intense and mutually satisfying safe sexual intercourse followed by a prolonged period of mature and fulfilling pillow talk.

As is plainly evident from this data there is quite a difference between a 'normal' man's constantly fluctuating levels, swinging from confident to chronic lack of confidence in a matter of a few minutes, and the reconstructed man's constantly increasing levels. The reconstructed man has a generally far higher and more stable reading and is only affected by outside negative stimuli (the article in the *Sydney Morning Herald*) rather than any internal negative feelings which will all have been removed through intensive analysis. So we can see that the role the analyst played in these men's lives has been vital.

There are however plenty of subjects around who have not taken this path, and I shall be looking at them later.

The Rise and Fall of the New Man

Of all the notions and ideas behind a male response to feminism, the 'New Man' was surely the most fake. As we have already seen, the term was anything but new, but this time round the glory was claimed by a man called Jasper Dunwoody who at the time was working for a large advertising agency.* He thought it would be a good way of selling bottled water and jeans, two accounts he was looking after. I'll let Jasper explain what he felt actually happened.

> It must have been about February 1980. I think, I know I was very excited about a lot of imagery that we were starting to look at. I can't remember where the original idea came from precisely, but basically, through networking, thousands of different ideas, I just came up with this concept. The New Man. In some ways it harked back to the Weimar Republic, you know, Bertold Brecht and that whole thing, but it was also saying something about the eighties. It shed the hippy image, it allowed sharply dressed men with good haircuts who knew where to buy consistently good knitwear to look after kids. It meant you didn't have to wear dungarees and a pair of those dreadful red Danish

* Jasper Dunwoody, balding, with ponytail, is now unemployed. His old employers, Bimshank, Garstang, Tupferberg were declared bankrupt on 30 June 1989 and he was laid off. He has never managed to find alternative employment and wishes he had learned some other 'skill' in his youth.

clogs, you could stand naked in your kitchen and express your sexuality by pouring a bottle of fairly exclusive mineral water over your flat-top hair cut and hold up a baby. Incredibly sexy image, women really went for it in a big way.

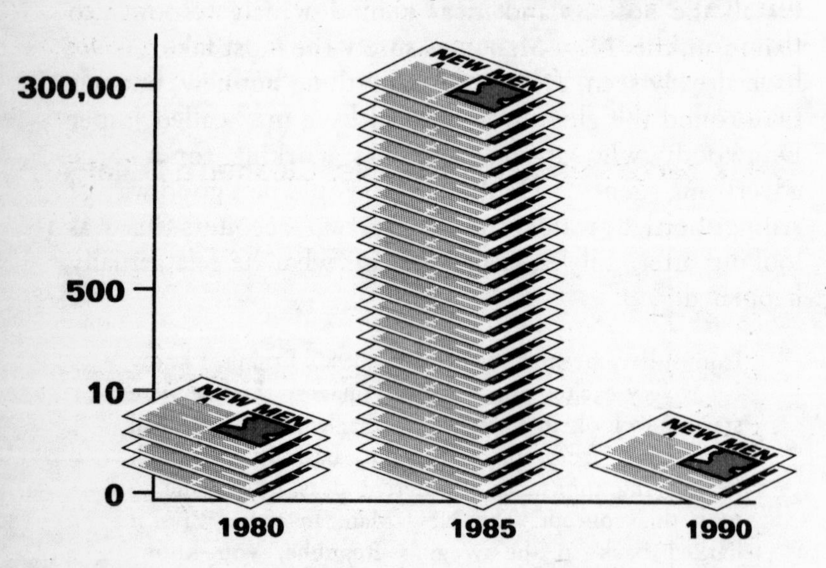

The notion of the New Man was immediately and enthusiastically picked up by the media. Between March 1980 and September 1989 there were over 30,000 articles about New Men printed in women's magazines. All these articles had question marks after the title. For instance: 'New Men, do we need them?' 'New Men, are they really different?' 'New Men, same Old opinions?' and 'Who gives a Twopenny Stuff about New Men?'

They supposedly proved the fact that there was a breed of man in existence who would willingly do their share of the housework and still look sexy in a torn white vest.

Research done by Professor Elaine Briggs of the Sheffield Polytechnic Sociological Statistics Study Group did some interesting research on the subject. She interviewed over 4,000 men in the relevant social groups, each of whom was asked 200 questions. One of the more eye-catching ones was, 'Have you ever cleaned a toilet bowl?' It was revealed that only 14% of men claimed ever to have cleaned a toilet bowl themselves. 78% stated they considered it strictly 'woman's work'.*

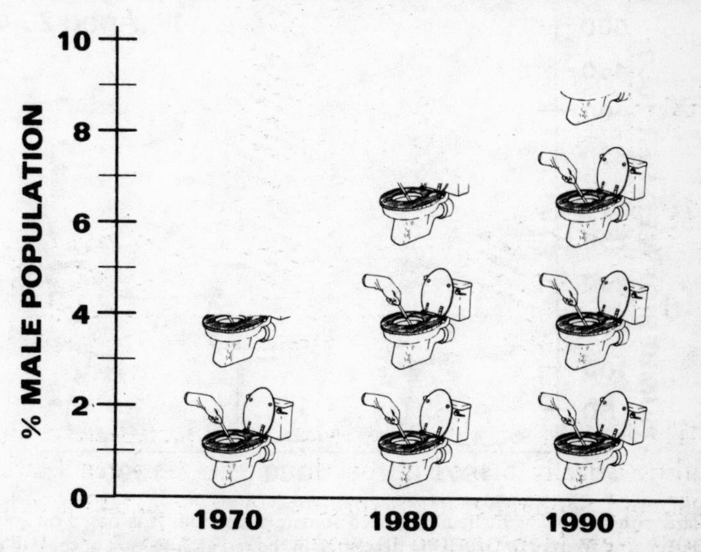

* Much of the data from the research has been put under a 'Section 13' restraining order under the Government's 50-year rule legislation. It has been very difficult to find out the official reasoning behind this, but leaked Whitehall sources have revealed that the results were pretty damning to our national masculine pride. It was feared a major depression could sweep the land resulting in untold millions of lost working hours.

Using these figures we have been able to project forward, and predict that by the year 2050 upwards of 25% of men in this country will have considered cleaning their own toilets, and some of them will actually have done so.

But the myth of the New Man was an attractive one. Advertising agencies pillaged the storehouse of homo-erotic images from the fifties. Young short-haired men with no shirts on, wearing torn jeans with the flies unbuttoned had, until the mid eighties, been strictly for the consumption of homosexual men and some upper class women.*

The advent of the 'new man' advert suddenly alerted

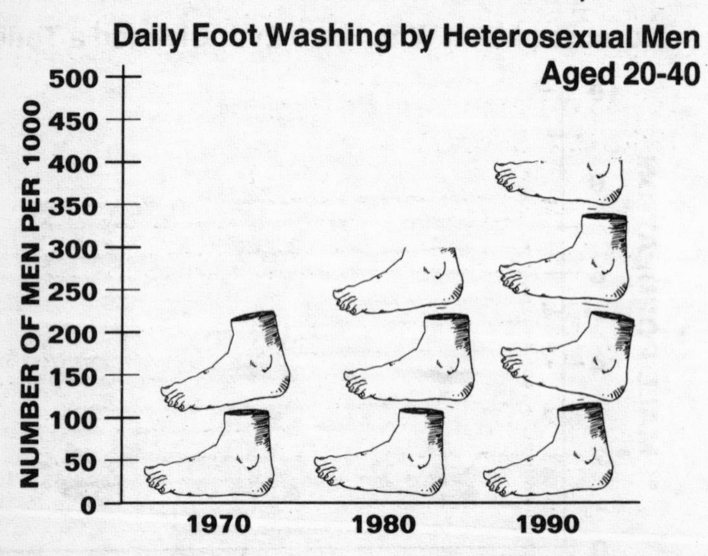

* This rather glib statement might need some explanation. It is based on solid research, the sources of which are described in the research section at the end of the book. Most of the upper class women I spoke to were forthright about 'getting terribly horny' at the sight of a young, well developed male torso. They would never consider marriage with such a man however, he was purely to be used for sexual gratification. They subscribed to the, 'I could get my nails into his buttocks, but the dolt will never get a ring on my finger' school of sexual philosophy.

straight men to the concept that they might possibly be judged by their bodies too. They might need to appear to be 'sexy' just as traditionally women have had to for centuries. Men realised they needed to prune and preen, in order to struggle for a place in the breeding market. Man as peacock is a tradition as old as the hills, but the Victorians combined with the First World War really put the kybosh on male vanity. That's why the advent of the New Man, even though he was 90% style, 0% content, 100% myth, had an impact.

By early 1990 the myth of the New Man was totally debunked, the sheer weight of critical magazine articles had killed it. Although some computer and mineral water companies were still using the naked-man-and-baby

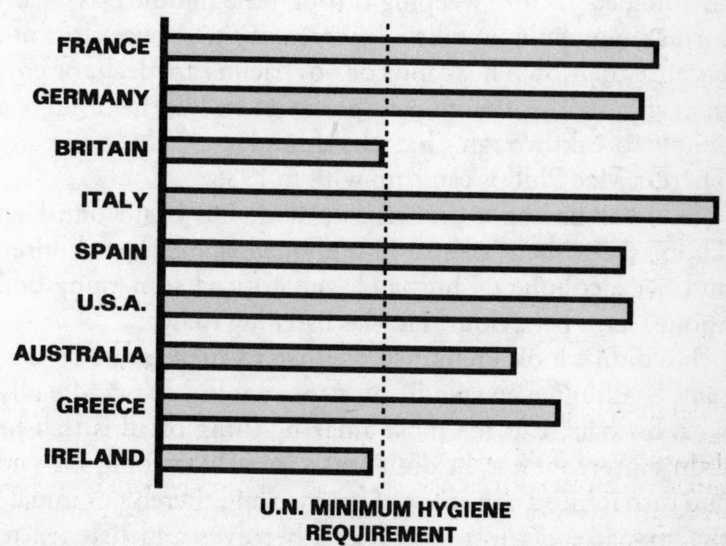

routine to push their products, the image had gone so out of fashion that it was ignored by the public and the campaigns flopped.

This, finally, takes us up to the first signs of reconstructed man emerging as a sociological phenomenon. One of the key events which helped shape my thesis took place on the West Coast of America.

The Designer Reconstructed Man

In California there is an escort agency called 'ManULike' which has seen a huge boom in business over the past four or five years. The boom is not due to any previously unspotted sociological factor sweeping through the middle class Californian women who take advantage of the service. It is not because their own husbands or boyfriends are dead, or gay, or even running off with younger women. It is the result of a simple breakthrough that the founder of the company Theresa Mae Philips came up with in 1986.

She was having a dinner date with her beau, one Dan Thomas. As she spoke to him about her life, her children and her alcoholic ex-husband, she noticed something odd about Dan's behaviour. He was listening to her.

He didn't look up and scan other women in the restaurant, he didn't even spindle his paper napkin or twiddle idly with his hair. But the most amazing thing of all is that he didn't interrupt her, he didn't take some little thing she said and turn it into a sob story of his own and thereby dominate the airspace. He just stared into her eyes and listened to every single word she had to say.

At first Theresa felt slightly dizzy and nauseous. After all she was, like most women the world over, used to listening to men, not being listened to by them. After a while she mentioned this to him and he smiled; he was embarrassed she'd noticed.

He finally admitted it was a simple trick he'd learned one night in a bar. All he had to do was stare into the woman's eyes and nod, adding sporadic murmurs of consent. It had proved to be, as he said, 'a sure fire way of getting a woman into the sack'.

After their sexual liaison had grown into an on going LTR,* she noticed that many of her women friends were very interested in what had happened to her. They wanted to know how come she was with a man and yet still happy. They had never seen anything like it before.

Then Theresa Mae had a brain-wave, she would set up an Escort agency with a difference. She went to Dan and asked him if he could teach other men the trick he'd shown her on that first night. He thought he could and the rest is history.

From the first advert to the first million took a mere six months. Within two years ManULike was turning over forty million dollars annually.† Theresa Mae Philips was featured on the front cover of Forbes Magazine in the Spring of 1989, under the banner headline, 'MEN SIT AND LISTEN WHILE I RAKE IN THE DOUGH!'

Whatever our opinions of Californian society, Theresa Mae Philips hit a raw nerve in the psyche of women when

* Living Together Relationship. A common replacement in California to conventional marriage, many people organise an elaborate 'LTR affirmation celebration' instead of a wedding party.

† There were tentative plans to start up a franchise in this country called 'Spud U Marry' but so far this has come to nothing.

LADIES, WE GUARANTEE YOU WILL RECEIVE

100%

ATTENTION ON YOUR DATE

FROM THE HAND PICKED MEN AT

CALL TOLL FREE, 24 HOURS 0112 991 8802

she set the company up. Women are so used to being ignored and spoken over that the simple fact of being listened to and taken seriously, must lead us to make one or two brash generalisations.

1 Normal men think they will turn into homosexuals if they listen to women.
2 Defensive men think that listening to women will confuse them even more and anyway it's not fair, women always natter on about something stupid.
3 Self-loathing men think listening to women could be seen as abysmal tokenist behaviour.

However if a reconstructed man were to hear of Theresa Mae Philips' discovery he would agree with her ideas and start to listen to everyone with amazing amounts of attentiveness and eye contact.

chapter 5

Day-to-Day Life: Q & A

So far I have looked at the background and development of what I classify as reconstructed men. In this next section I want to look in more detail at reconstructed behaviour and attitudes as they manifest themselves in our day-to-day lives. I want to give women readers helpful hints and tips on spotting a reconstructed man, and if she is so inclined, getting him into bed and keeping him there long enough to develop something akin to a long-term growth-oriented relationship.

However, male readers shouldn't be put off by this, because of the depth of my research, they may also, by default as it were, pick up some useful tips on being picked up by today's modern woman.*

During my lecture tours I have been asked thousands of questions about reconstructed men, their behaviour and effect on society. What I have tried to do here is answer the most commonly asked questions and use testimony from my study group to highlight key issues.

* As we shall see later in the section on courting, it is generally speaking, the woman who now makes the first move.

Q: How Do You Spot a Reconstructed Man?

A: This isn't as hard as it might sound. Reconstructed men tend to occur in fairly predictable professions. You are unlikely to meet a reconstructed butcher, soldier, arms manufacturer, taxi driver or heavy metal musician. You are likely to meet one who works in the media, the arts, local government, the social services, architecture, psycho-analysis and of course, graphic design.

He is likely to be over thirty and he will have given up a very wide array of activities: smoking, heavy drinking, hard drug use, pornography and male bonding camaraderie based on language found offensive by women.

Spotting reconstructed men is, therefore, a little easier than it might at first appear. Once you have spotted one you may find that life becomes a little more difficult.

Q: Where Might You Meet a Reconstructed Man?

A: As women begin to understand the concept of reconstruction, they often feel that there is no physical proof for them to grapple with. They want to know where they might actually meet a reconstructed man, what sort of environment does he feel at home in.

This may be the key to the problem, because the one environment he does feel at home in is the home. He is not likely to be hanging around a singles bar, a wine bar or a public bar. He might be found in a tapas bar on rare occasions, or even hanging from a chin-up bar in a gymnasium, but he won't be in the normal places women might expect 'men on the loose' to congregate.

There is no easy answer. Gymnasia, garden centres and crèches are all a good start, but he is just as likely to be in a nice rural pub which does good food or on a long-distance cycle ride with a mixed group of environmentalists.

I felt the only way to find out was to ask some reconstructed men where their partners had met them, and where they spent a lot of their free time. Simon Greatrex told me this:

> I try to undermine the hierarchy at my architecture company by cooking lunch for the staff one day a week. Reanna was one of the guests one time. She thought I was the caterer and treated me accordingly, I found her very attractive but said nothing. When it was finally revealed that I was the boss, the status confusion she experienced obviously worked to my advantage. She was very apologetic, having committed a social blunder. I made little of it, claiming to find it charming. We've been together ever since.

Gerald Milligan had a very different approach. It seems he actually sat down and devised a plan which would help him find what he referred to as a 'life partner'.

> I spent many hours pondering this problem with my male friends. We didn't seem to meet women with whom we felt comfortable. I eventually decided on a lateral approach. I trained as a nanny and applied for jobs with high powered single women with young children. Before long I was involved in eight separate complex relationships with these women. It was a hectic time of my life. I finally narrowed the field until I settled on one, with whom I've been in a delightful and child-producing relationship ever since.

Obviously this isn't going to help all women, especially if they are looking for a responsible man with whom to start producing offspring. The best way seems to be the mushroom hunter's method, which, although it possibly sounds a little hippyish, has proved to be very successful. Ray Hogthorne explains how he trains people during his 'mushroom-hunting as life-skills' expeditions.

> We start out walking along a set route, and everybody is told to look hard for mushrooms. We walk along staring at the ground, looking under leaves, poking things with sticks. We find one, maybe two mushrooms, that's it. Then we give up, turn around and head for home. We use the same route on the way back. No mention is made of mushrooms, people walk and talk freely. They immediately start to find mushrooms, hundreds of mushrooms, right where we had walked only half an hour before.

I think it's pretty clear the message we're getting from Mr Hogthorne. Basically, the more you look, the more effort you expend in searching for a reconstructed man, the less chance you will have of finding one.

Q: Are Reconstructed Men More Complex?

A: Reconstructed men are far more complicated than their forefathers. For them, all statements conceal many deep layers of subtext which they feel a duty to be keenly aware of. No longer will your moods go unnoticed, you new jewellery un-commented on, your new hairstyle un-appraised. You may though, find that not all the comments are glib flattery. All your actions will be invested with meaning and importance.

If, for instance, you have just paid a great deal of money for a root perm and you meet your reconstructed beau, he may well say: '*Your hair, it's different.*'

This might please you and you will explain no doubt how long it took, adding one or two amusing anecdotes about your time at the hairdressers and how well you get on with very camp gay men. You may notice however that he is still looking at your hair from different angles and assessing its shape and his emotional responses to it. You may then receive a comment like this: '*I like it initially, but I feel, and I mean this in a supportive way, that you have lost something of the simple charm that I, and a lot of men I know, found attractive in you.*'

You will still, no doubt, be feeling okay. You will then explain how you felt like a change, it's made you feel better about yourself, you can now go on with your life in a new and exciting direction. As you speak, if you see him nodding vigorously, you know that this body language agreement with your statements is softening you up for the final onslaught. He will make the sporadic murmer of consent 'mmm' sound a few times. Then, after a short silence will possibly come out with something along the lines of: '*I'm not saying you look cheap or* nouveau riche *exactly, but it has to be said that many women who appear in a topless capacity in the more popular daily newspapers tend to choose a similar style. That is not to say the style is inherently wrong, but it is saying something about you. The effort shows and people will read it. They will think, "look at her, she's had her hair done and it means something". That's all I'm saying.*'*

* This interaction was recorded during one of my seminars where I used an actor well-versed in advanced reconstructed psychology to respond to a woman in the class who was sporting a new hair-do. The mini psycho-drama sparked a three hour discussion on the beauty industry and its hold over women.

If by now, you are still managing to experience that warm inner feeling of self-love that you first felt as you caught sight of your reflection in a shop window, you may well be able to survive a long-term commitment with a reconstructed man.

Q: If a Man Does the Washing Up, Is It Safe to Assume He's Reconstructed?

A: This question has come up a surprising number of times. For some reason the cliché has become a sociological fact of life. The '*oh, he's ever so good around the house, he always does the washing up*' has become a way through the minefield of accusations and dissatisfactions that many men have found. Doing the washing up, the normal man surmises, is a small price to pay for a bit of peace and quiet. John Blake:

> I started washing up in 1972, after the wife read an article in *Woman's Realm* about how it's not fair that women have to do all the housework. She was giving me ear ache for months about how I came in from work, sat my fat arse in front of the telly as she said, and never lifted a finger. Blimey, she's got a mouth on her, that one. Anyway, I tried telling her I was tired from being the breadwinner, but she was working full time as well, so that argument turned to dust as I stood there. So I worked it out. Do the washing up, just leave it on the drainer, doesn't take long and it'll keep her happy. She still has to do all the shopping, laundry, hoovering, ironing, sort out the bills, re-decorate the house and make the bed, oh, and clean the bog of course, you wouldn't catch me doing that.

So, watching a man do the washing up is no proof of anything. In fact a reconstructed man could well hold back from doing any domestic chores for a time, particularly at the opening stages of a relationship. Gerald Milligan gives his two-penn'orth:

> When I first started seeing Mary on a regular basis I let her do all the domestic work. If I went to her place for dinner, I didn't lift a finger. After a while she confronted me with this. She said something like, 'I thought you were supposed to be right on, how come you never do anything around the house? You're worse than my old boyfriend, at least he did the washing up.' It was classic. I explained that her old boyfriend was mollifying her and not challenging the old patriarchal power base in any way. I on the other hand was not ploughing into her kitchen, invading her space, taking over as it were. I was biding my time and waiting for the relationship to develop before I started to negotiate any possible role I may have in what was, after all, her domestic territory. She did apparently, wonder how long this assessment period was going to be, as by that time we'd regularly been seeing each other for five years. I suppose she had a point. I started doing the washing up that night I think.

The basic answer to the question is, no, it is not safe to assume anything. A fully reconstructed man should find it quite hard to allow a woman to do anything in the domestic realm, because, as we shall see in a later chapter, a major power shift is taking place in our private, as well as our public lives.

Q: Will a Woman be Socially Embarrassed by a Reconstructed Man?

A: Over the centuries many women have spent their lives in a state of perpetual social embarrassment over the hopeless social blunderings of their male partners.

They have sat in pubs wondering how they can love this man who is holding forth so confidently at the bar, oblivious of the fact that the people around him are yawning and glancing at their watches. They can introduce him to their women friends and he will immediately dominate the conversation by explaining to them in detail how he can drive safely when he's very drunk.

Levels of Social Embarrassment in Women Caused by 'Normal' Male Behaviour

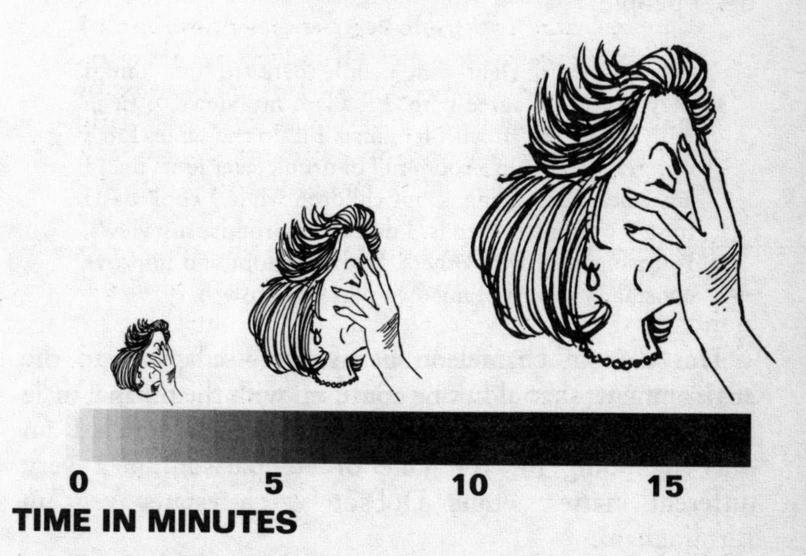

As we can see from this graph which results from tests run by the Social Embarrassment Study Group of Swindon Polytechnic, women are deeply affected by their partner's attitudes. The shading along the bottom represents the woman's facial blushing. We can see her appraisal of the situation goes from bad to worse over a fifteen-minute period.

A reconstructed man will not do this, he is far more sensitive and aware of his surroundings and the differing opinions and tastes of people he meets. He does not assume that all his opinions are correct at all times in all circumstances. He sees opinions in a more fluid organic way, constantly growing and changing. The chameleon could perhaps be the mascot of the reconstructed man.

I asked study group member Matthew Carlton, a well reconstructed man, about how he avoids embarrassing other people:

> When I'm with right-wing people there are some things they say I will agree with, I'll adapt my views to fit in with theirs. If I'm with feminists I'll do the same. I'm a different person in a room full of drunk lager louts than I am when I'm talking about children while I cook pasta for a few women friends. I don't compromise my views, I just blend in with others. I adapt, adopt and improve constantly as part of my own personal growth.

This sort of chameleon behaviour – adapting to the environment – shouldn't be confused with the normal male habit of living with double standards. This, which I am only including for the sake of comparison, is a very different matter. Frank Dobson is an estate agent in Birmingham.

> I came home to find the eldest son in bed with some floozy piece. I was appalled. The wife could have come in, she'd have had a turn. I gave him a piece of my mind and gave the young madam a right talking to. Lovely figure though, I suppose I should have let her get dressed before I told her off but it's not often a man my age gets an eye-full like that.

Another, seemingly very common area of social embarrassment can loosely be called 'ogling other women'. If, for example, two couples go out to dinner, and, at a certain point in the evening, one of the (normal) men spots a young woman entering the restaurant, he would probably lean close to his male friend and whisper surreptitiously to the other something along the lines of: '*I could slip her a portion, no problem chief, I'm rock hard.*'

This would, of course, be the cause of much suppressed mirth among the men, the source of which would never be revealed to the women, who were both supposedly under the impression that their men 'weren't like that'.

The reconstructed man would never engage in this sort of behaviour. In the unlikely event that he even bothered to notice a woman he didn't know entering a restaurant who he found sexually attractive, he wouldn't, as some might expect, pretend he didn't notice her.

If questioned about her he would merely state that visually he certainly found her highly stimulating, but he couldn't get more sexually excited until he knew her personally, and as he had no intention of getting to know her, further discussion of her attributes, either social or sexual was pointless.

Some women find this hard to believe as it would look as though he were ogling the stranger in just the same manner as any man she has ever known.

Q: How Do You Get a Reconstructed Man into a Long-Term Growth-Oriented Relationship?

A: In the course of my work, many people ask me how a woman should go about actually getting a reconstructed man into a long-term growth-oriented relationship. This is not a question I, as a man, like to answer, but for the sake of science I will do my best.

Once a woman has decided, preferably after in-depth consultation with her analyst or psychotherapist, that the reconstructed man is the appropriate choice for her, she needs to remember a few things.

As we have already discussed, his heart has been dissected and reconstructed so thoroughly, normal courting procedures are simply not suitable. Playing romantic games is simply impossible – he knows all actions and statements are imbued with layers of subtext. A simple question to him such as: '*Are you doing anything on Tuesday night?*' will result in a response along the lines: '*If your motives are sexual, I will have to adjust to seeing you in a new light. If not, then a social date with a member of the opposite sex is a broadening and worthwhile option.*' A fairly deadening response I think you'll agree.

If, to counter this, you suggest something like: '*I was only trying to make things romantic,*' he will almost certainly respond with the reconstructed theory which runs: '*Romance is encouraged by governments to keep people busy with their own private lives, thereby ignoring the oppressive political regime. I'm trying to remove this system of blinkers in order to maintain more open and honest relationships and challenge the present government.*'

If you're still awake, it's probably best to nod and go along with it all or walk away as quickly as you can and hope he doesn't notice.

Another suggestion is to try approaching him on a purely logical level. One where you explain the mutual benefits of forming a partnership where you are both aware of the pitfalls of Victorian romanticism. The more clinical and compartmentalised your approach, the more he may find room for impetuous behaviour. I asked Peter Bradshaw about the time he was courted by his long-term partner.

> She informed me by fax that genetically I looked like a good match from a long-term breeding point of view. I found this very stimulating and responded by sending her a book on Japanese Cinema. The note attached informed her that I didn't want her to take the gift in a demeaning way, but if she was willing to enter negotiations with a view to intercourse, I was hot, hard and ready.

It is not that a reconstructed man will be incapable of wild and passionate longing. But he will have experienced the negative side of this behaviour before he went through the process of growth to self-knowledge; he will have led a chaotic and wild life for many years before finally starting to sort it out.

Social worker Richard Green told me he had almost achieved this state:

> Our relationship was so perfect, we even had our sexual routine worked out months in advance. I eventually felt like we needed more spontaneity but I held back because of the danger of infringing on each other's personal space. Now we are working towards an agreement

where we will have pre-arranged 'spontaneity periods' once each month, where just about anything can happen.

Q: Once I've Got Him There, What Will He Be Like?

A: A very common question. We have seen from statistical research on the subject that he is more likely to clean the toilet, change the nappies and wash the kitchen floor than his forebears, but is that all there is to it?

From my interviews, it would seem this is only the start. Recent research on the way our public and private lives are being enacted shows how some remarkable changes are taking place under our noses. Women are slowly but surely making a bigger and bigger impact on the work force. They are still working harder, being paid less and being badly treated for their efforts, but there is no denying the swing. There are plenty of sad old King Canutes both on the left and the right in politics who are trying to stem the tide, but they are on a losing wicket and will soon be swept away by history.

However it's important to remember there's no such thing as a free clean kitchen. Although reconstructed men are masters at relinquishing power in public life – i.e. they think women should be police chiefs, politicians, judges and brain surgeons – they believe that as a consequence men are going to have to take over to some degree in the home.

Reconstructed men don't do 'their share' of the washing up, or put the rubbish out and empty the hoover bag. They run the entire operation. They are the forerunners of the male/female power shift which is presently taking place in our society. As women slowly become more and more powerful in public life (note the appointment of the new director of public prosecutions) so men will start to become more powerful in the home.

Geoffrey Fachetti has 'swapped roles' for three years, and his life has changed dramatically because of this:

> I was brought up like any man, never considering the aesthetics of the domestic environment as it were. When Kate got the new job, and we were faced with having full-time professional child care for Griselda and Henson, well, I just said no. Kate thought I was doing some revisionist number, she thought I wanted her back in the home, barefoot and pregnant, chained to the kitchen sink. I told her I would throw in the towel at the practice* and take up the house, full time. Kate laughed, but soon got used to it. I admit the transition period was difficult, I didn't feel at home in the house. All the decorations were Kate's, all the ideas for curtains, where the furniture went, everything had been her decision. I'd always said 'Whatever you like darling', pretty typical really. Well, I started to change everything, I eventually had the whole house gutted and lined in oak panelling, leather Chesterfields, old books and a couple of Civil war muskets over the roaring fire. It cost a bomb and Kate went up the wall, but she swallowed it eventually. I love the house now, so do the kids; it has a great, dark, musty masculine feel to it, and I think both my daughters are benefitting from it. Kate can't stand it, but she's hardly ever here what with work pressures.

It seems as though all the minutiae of the roles are reversed as well as the major areas. From what I could tell,

* Geoffrey was a surveyor.

Kate became more and more remote at home, not seeming to make contact with the children. The tables were eventually completely turned when Geoffrey found out Kate was having an affair with her secretary, a twenty-four-year-old beef-cake called Mitch. As far as I know they worked it out and are still together.*

As we can see, though, many reconstructed men enjoy domestic work; basic cooking and cleaning activities give them time to daydream. These dreams usually consist of complex sexual fantasies which raise the male libido to previously undreamed of heights. As Jack Abrahams, one of my study group told me

> After doing the hoovering, I'm horny like a butcher's dog. I usually time it so I've finished when Sally gets back in from the office. I explain my latest dream and we start a very high energy sex session which can sometimes last five or six hours.

So we can see here that a house-husband isn't necessarily going to be some asexual being in a frilly apron. Far more likely his apron will be covering an almost constantly rampant member. It seems that if anything, the sex life of the nation will improve as we shall see in the next chapter.†

The low level of tension in the man increases his ability to perform sexually over a longer period. We can see in this graph the relative lengths of time men in various

* See next section on reconstructed responses to this event.

† That's the sex chapter, the one which I have found, statistically, a lot of people read first. However I have put it at the back of the book for a good reason. I have discovered that a lot of reconstructed men save up sexual activity as a 'treat' after they have finished the domestic chores. It is a fairly common sexual fantasy for him to be hoovering or emptying the rubbish, knowing his partner is in bed, warm and relaxed, reading a heavy duty sexual political masterwork.

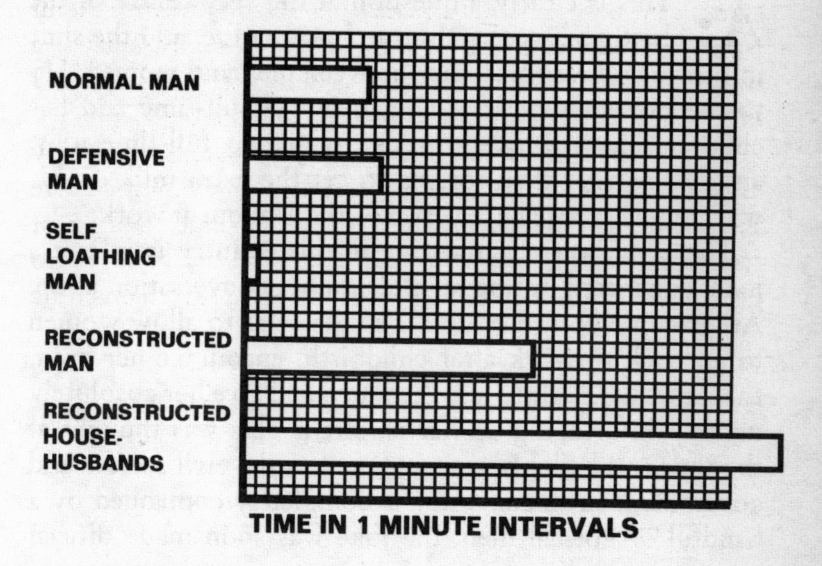

professions are able to maintain a respectable erection and not climax.

This sort of information, when it becomes common knowledge, is going to greatly increase the attraction that many reconstructed house-husbands will have. It is predicted by specialists in the field that by the year 2000, millions of women in developed countries will want their men to give up full time work once the children are born, and this is going to have a drastic but possibly beneficial effect on industry and commerce.

Q: The Reconstructed Father – Will He Help?

A: This is clearly a question at the very centre of the battle between public and private life, and the shift in power and responsibility between men and women. Up to the present day, if a woman works full-time and has children, she effectively holds down two full-time jobs, and her partner then forgets to get the extra milk on his way home because he had a lot to think about at work.

The provision of child-care in this country is in fact a joke, concocted during an after-dinner conversation at the Atheneum club in London. The idea was to allow women to go back to work after childbirth, encourage her even, then, pay her slightly less than men and give her absolutely no help in bringing up her children. This was thought at the time to be highly amusing, and as the civil service and government in this country is completely controlled by a handful of normal men, the joke was soon made official government policy.

There are more pre-school child-care facilities in Portugal, one of the poorest countries in the EC than there are in Britain, where we cater for just 2.5% of our pre-school children, when the demand is something around 78%. In France for example, they have facilities for 120% of their children, which is a typical showy French thing to do.

Normal men have not changed their working habits or attitudes to child-care one click since 1958. It's still considered a woman's work, as Barry Titchfield states:

> It's a mothers job, isn't it. Kids need a mum to look after them. Wouldn't be natural if I did it. I'd feel a right lemon walking along the street pushing a pram. What

> about my manhood? No, that's her territory. You wouldn't catch me having anything to do with my pack of brats. I love 'em of course, as long as they leave me alone to watch the footy.

The reconstructed attitude is bound to be different, but I didn't realise quite how different until I spoke to Colin Hibbert. Colin was very involved with his children, right from the very start.

> Patty's pregnancy hit me for six. I got back ache, morning sickness, the works. I got food obsessions just before she did. I'd come home one day with a huge bag of peaches and she'd be delighted. She'd tell me all she could think about was peaches. I'd explain to her that the peaches were for me, I felt the same. Then the birth itself was fantastic. I'd been to all the ante-natal classes. Patty couldn't make many of them because of her work but I knew what to do. I was showing her the breathing technique, and I got so into the pushing that I somehow pulled a muscle in my pelvic floor and I tore. It was very painful. I had to be rushed to casualty to have four stitches. Patty didn't have any, she was fine.

Colin now looks after his own three children full time while his wife Patty does 'something in the city'. He explains how this works out.

> I gave up work as soon as Francesca was born. Patty went back to work pretty quick, and I've been home ever since. I'd done a lot of child-care before we had our own kids, mainly because I wanted to be sure I could do it. I was a nanny for three years with a really obnoxious French family, the husband was a diplomat here. Lovely kids though, and I had an affair with his wife, but that's

> another story. By the time my own kids came along, it was second nature. None of this, 'I don't know how to change a nappy' business with me. In fact I teach at the post-natal classes down at St Luke's three times a week.

It's clear from what Colin has said then that within a reconstructed relationship, in this case a role reversal one, it is more likely for the woman to 'help' with the child-care and the man to be the main nurturer.

Reconstructed men are aware that they are generally in a uniquely privileged position, being in relationships with wealthy women. Nigel Moreton was quite mercenary when it came to starting a family.

> I met Wendy at a dinner party. She was a barrister, and I immediately took a fancy to her. As we had coffee and After Eights, I cornered her and told her that I would willingly look after her children if she wanted to keep going to work. She informed me she didn't have any children, and that was when I suggested we make them. I now live in a £500,000 town house, I have my own car, a country cottage and an allowance of £850 a week. I look after our two lovely children and run my own consultancy business from home. I know I'm lucky, and I do a lot of charity work with unmarried mothers. But why any man wants a job is quite, quite beyond me.

This sort of attitude greatly upsets defensive men who often feel trapped by their jobs, mortgages and responsibilities. Barry Thompson is one such example, married for eight years, three children and a suburban house.

> All the hours God sends I'm in the office. I slog my bloody guts out trying to make ends meet, and I get

> home to a barrage of accusations that I'm sexist and boring and the fact that my dick's too small. It makes you sick. All her poxy girlfriends are there, in the kitchen, slagging me off because I never do any housework. I'm never in the bloody house, that's why. Chance would be a fine thing. I've started getting pissed a lot like my dad!

As we might expect a self-loathing man has a different opinion. Frank Jessop is a married self-loathing man who tries harder than most to pull his weight.

> I'm so useless. I was changing Rupert's nappy the other day, I'd been up all night with Sarah, and I forgot to put powder on Rupert's sore bum. Kate screamed at me for being incompetent. I just stood there crying until she pushed me out of the way. I think I should do more to help with the kids but I always seem to make a mess, so Kate throws me out and does it herself. I expect I do it badly to get out of it which is so sly and male. It's sickening isn't it, when you can see it, but you can't really do anything about it.

Q: How Does a Reconstructed Man React When He Discovers His Partner is Having an Affair?

A: I was once asked this question at the end of one of my lectures. The man who asked me looked charming, quite possibly deeply reconstructed in his own way. The woman who sat next to him, obviously an open and aware human being, was suddenly overcome with guilt-based emotions and started staring at the floor. It was clear that this couple was dealing with some pretty full-on challenges to their complacent lifestyle.*

All the way through the book I have been looking at ways in which normal and reconstructed men lie, cheat and con their way through life. Here I was faced with a whole new set of problems, and I was fascinated to find out what reconstructed men did on these occasions. First I asked Matthew Carlton if he'd ever had a similar experience.

> I can't really imagine it. It could only mean I had gone wrong somewhere, I had failed to satisfy some need in my partner and I would find that a pretty devastating notion. I also believe I would be open, sensitive and aware enough to see it coming a mile off. As soon as I did, I would take some affirmative action.

A classic reconstructed response, and a very common one amongst the reconstructed study group. As a matter of interest, the normal response was very varied. John Blake didn't react completely according to type when I asked him about his wife's infidelity.

> Well, what can you do, I'm off on the road six days a week. I'm not saying I don't wander down the by-ways and what have you, so I can't complain really. I suppose if I found her actually, well, you know, in flagrante whatsit I'd do me nut. I'd have to sort the bloke out good and proper. Well, I wouldn't do it, but I'd get my

* When I use the term complacent here, I don't mean it as a sly put-down. It has been discovered that all heterosexual couples reach a state of inner complacency after about one year. Perfectly normal, and if handled correctly, perfectly harmless.

> mate Barry round, he's well hard. Come to think of it, Barry's often at my place when I get home as it is. Well, there you go, who'd have thought it, Barry, my best mate. What a bastard. Right under my nose.

This confused attitude seems to be very common in contemporary relationships. So many of the old rules which governed our lives have broken down, many people don't know which ones to follow and which to ignore. Following the heart would seem to be correct, but as many reconstructed men know, this can certainly make one appear to be following very traditional 'woman as chattel' lines of behaviour.

Tom Drybell, a thirty-three-year-old teacher explained how he dealt with the news of external sexual liaisons carried out by Mary, his partner of seven years:

> We were having one of our 'get down to brass tacks' type discussions. Mary had just smashed a plate over my head and told me to 'stop being so sodding reasonable'. I thought this was fair enough and told her I could see her point of view. She kept going on and on about how she loved Pete, how his dick was bigger and harder and how she was seeing him as often as she could. I thought that logically, that seemed fair enough although I did have a lump in my throat which I took to be a more subconscious emotional response, probably self-pity, so I ignored it.

Tom was dealing with this trauma very well, although he chewed his lips so badly he needed medical treatment, he never once raised his voice and never resorted to violence. Through workshops and discussions with friends he eventually came to the realisation that he did love Mary enough to follow her and confront her lover. This he did. He takes up the story again.

> I rang on the door-bell about ten minutes after she'd gone in. This man opened the door, he seemed very nice and I was relieved she wasn't seeing some ruffian. I explained who I was, making plenty of non-threatening signals that I'd learned in a workshop. Plenty of out-turned palms, smiles, raised eyebrows and prolonged eye contact. It seemed to work and soon Pete and I were getting on very well. Mary wasn't too happy about this and stormed off in a huff. Pete and I now spend a lot of time together; I've even baby-sat for his young son Toby. Mary and I are back together, and I think once she gets over the immense feelings of resentment and bitterness she has towards me, we will get along like we used to. Although she has been out late quite often recently.

If a woman is going to have an extra-marital affair, she is far better off with a reconstructed husband. He'll never turn up outside their love nest with a sawn-off shot gun – it's far more likely that he'll talk for hours through the letter-box until they have had enough and give up.

Q: If the Relationship Breaks Down, How Does a Reconstructed Man React?

A: Even in the most enlightened of relationships, things can go wrong, and keep going wrong until both parties begin to get the feeling that maybe this thing is over. Huge waves of guilt and despair overwhelm them, they cannot see life going on without their partner, but they cannot see how they can stay together.

There are many reasons why relationships break down, but I want to look in particular at the way reconstructed men cope with the stress and strain imposed on them when this takes place – the way men and women see the failure of relationships may point to some of the reasons for the break-up in the first place.

Below we can see two illustrations of how this break-up is envisioned. The first is done by a woman, the head of a local authority cleansing department.

The second was done by her husband, he is a social worker and house-husband.

Gerald Milligan is now involved in his third MTR* and

Male View of Relationship Break-up

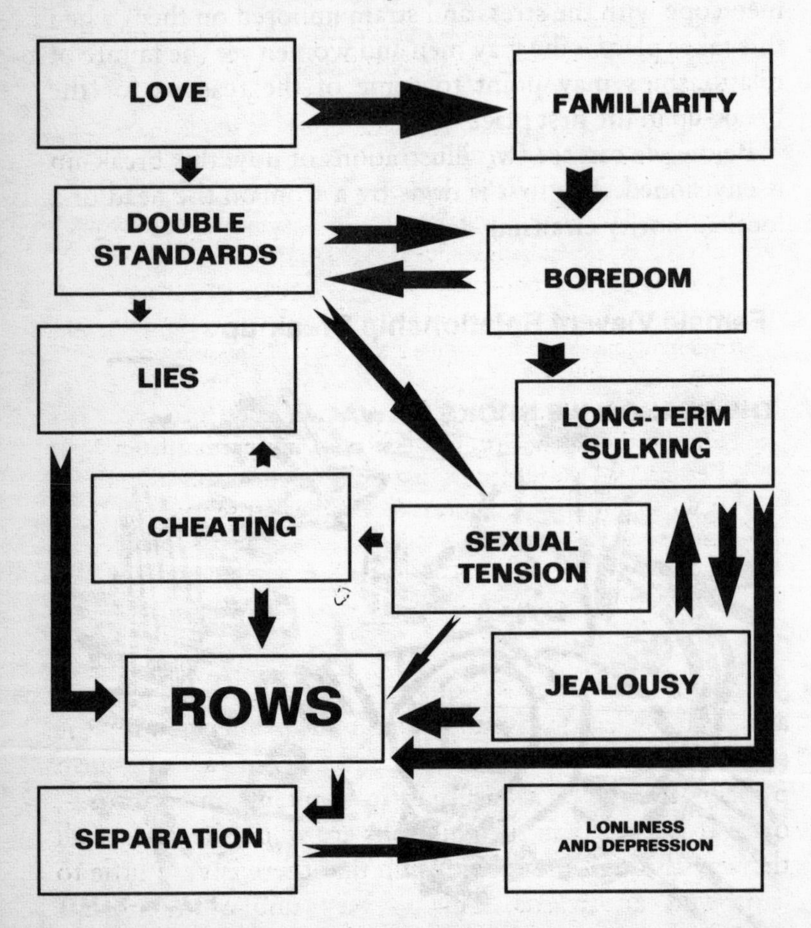

* An MTR is Gerald's own particular classification. Marriage Type Relationship. i.e. he lives with the woman but they haven't been through the 'mythical Victorian institution of sexist and oppressive vows' together.

has therefore been through two fairly prolonged and difficult break-ups. As a very highly reconstructed man, I was interested to know how Gerald coped. He was only too willing to tell me.

> The split with Reanna was a particularly difficult period. We were both very strong personalities, and when we clashed, well, our friends have since told us, they kept well out of it for fear of physical injury. I think that's going a bit far, I never hit her, well, I pushed her off after she had shoved my head into the gas oven and set fire to my hair. When we finally split I had to spend a great deal of time at friends' houses, talking. Mainly sitting at their kitchen tables running my hands through what was left of my hair and explaining in minute detail every last moment of our relationship. I was very depressed, but I kept on talking, it was very cathartic. I was also extremely sexually charged, very libidinally focussed. One of the interesting side-effects of my parting from Reanna was we started having really good sex together. It was a way of healing the pain. All the best sex we ever had together the really good sex, amazing, passionate and kinky sex, all happened after we split up and we stole odd afternoons together.

I have come across this phenomenon many times amongst the reconstructed men I have interviewed, the sudden overwhelming sexual interest in a long-term partner after the relationship is, to all intents and purposes, over. It is as though the emotions are so on the surface all the way through the relationship that there is very little to 'sort out' afterwards. This is very unlike the normal experience, and just for contrast I include this interview with John Blake about his divorce.

> We never talked much in the nine years we were married, but when the bitch left she screwed me for every penny she could get. I had to sell the house, the car, you know, usual goings on, you don't want to hear. I was out on a limb, living in a bedsit on my own. I had to keep up a front, well you have to don't you. People don't want to know. They've got troubles of their own. So I was all smiles at work, all my mates at the pub never knew a thing about it. They never asked, I never told them. It was okay. I only cried myself to sleep for the first three years, now I hardly ever do.

It seems to be clear that the normal man finds any expression of his emotions embarrassing and degrading, whereas by contrast, some reconstructed men feel embarrassed if they don't have a surfeit of emotional baggage to carry, as Nigel Rundle told me:

> Tom and Graham were both going through very difficult relationship break-ups and were so, well, so rich with emotion. That's the only way I can describe it. I used to sit with them for hour after hour, listening to their tales. They had terrible fights, marathon crying, loving and fighting sessions. Great rich swathes of emotion. They'd eventually ask me how I was getting on with Anna. I'd tell them everything was fine, we were really happy, the kids were fine, you know. Then they'd look at me as though I had no life. It was devastating. So I started fighting with Anna. Slagging her off and making her cry for no reason. I felt terrible about it because I love her, but Tom and Graham were really impressed, I was accepted back into the fold, as it were, not that I function in a way whereby I need male approval, well, not much.

Q: Is the Married Reconstructed Man a Good Partner for an Illicit Affair?

A: I have discussed this issue with various women over the last twenty years and come to numerous rock solid conclusions. Now, without wanting to take a moral stand, I feel it is important to describe what a lot of these women thought about this issue.*

Basically, if you are the sort of person who likes to go out with married men, you should perhaps look at the whole way you operate within society. You might need to evaluate your attitudes both towards yourself as a person, and towards the family group within which the man resides. The family is now far more commonly seen as a social construct which, being conducted in a post-feminist era, is possibly not as invalid and negative a force as was previously assumed.†

However, that said, if you are going to indulge in a non-committed liaison with a married man, then without doubt a reconstructed married man is by far the best bet. If you get tangled up with a normal one, it can be a very depressing experience as Wally Tamworth, a normal member of my study group relates.

* It may be thought that I am using these women as a shield to hide behind while I make rash, right-wing statements about the sanctity of the family. I can only defend myself by saying I have been a fierce and vociferous opponent of the family unit as we have known it in the past, but also a keen explorer for new ways in which we could live together. I hope that lets me off any possible hooks.

† This is speaking strictly within the boundaries of heterosexuality. There are, of course, as we all know, or should know, still very profound arguments from the gay community about the heterosexual cultural hegemony and disenfranchisement caused by the heterosexual family unit as a building block of social repression.

> It was a bit of an ego boost that a girl her age was willing to do it with a bloke like me. I told her I loved her, seemed to help really, you know, she was more willing to go all the way. Then she got all serious, I'd go round to her place and all she wanted to do was talk. She knew I was married with kiddies but she wanted the works. She wanted wedding bells. I'll tell you what, wedding bells, more like bloody alarm bells mate. I was out of there like a flash. Whoosh. You couldn't see me for dust mate. I had to dump her. Shame really.

As we have seen already, a reconstructed man's attitude is a little more sympathetic and understanding. He will never tell you he's fallen in love with you in order to gain sexual favours. He'll never compare you to his wife, never expect you to stop what you are doing and leave with him for a fantasy life of hedonism on a desert island. Donald Wallace, the architect we met earlier, explains how he has affairs.

> When I become involved in a sexual interaction outside the confines of marriage, I see what is happening as a simple friendship built around a sporting or leisure pursuit. I have affairs in much the same way other people play golf. I don't expect my wife would be interested in golf, so I don't expect her to show any interest in my other activities. I don't tell her about it and we all remain on a fairly level-headed footing.

When the excitement finally leaves the illicit affair, the woman will find a reconstructed man has an excellent attitude to the whole thing. He will not be burdened with guilt in the same way as his normal brother. He will still be able to acknowledge you publicly, he may, in some very advanced circumstances, be prepared to introduce you to his wife.

Q: Do Reconstructed Men Support the Backlash Against Feminism?

A: The simple answer to this question is of course no. The backlash is clearly a phenomenon of the defensive male, a man who feels under threat from the women who surround him professionally and privately. These men are often journalists working for what can loosely be dubbed the Tory press. They are usually short in stature, mild in manner and frightened in the office. They see the women around them becoming slightly more powerful and translate this fear on to a world stage. They will write, 'all career women are becoming powerful, ball-breaking harpies', when one woman in one newspaper office has told him to 'piss off' when he's said, 'make us a coffee would you pet?'

This is not to imply that these men are powerless, they have the ear of the nation, and if they start writing, 'feminism has failed, single career-women are lonely, miserable, childless and infertile' for long enough, people will start to believe it. They do need to be seen in context though. I have described defensive men in quite some detail as they are often portrayed as 'the' male response to feminism, when in fact they are only a tiny minority of rather outspoken men who generally have a string of disastrous and unresolved relationships in their past. The break-down of these relationships will generally be seen to be the women's fault (see blame re-alignment).

I asked a defensive man, Bill Quantock, what he thought about the backlash.

> At last, women are getting some of their own medicine. Feminism isn't working is it? Women who dedicate themselves to their careers are all lonely and depressed. See how they like it, I've been lonely and depressed for years. I mean, let's face it, women just can't do everything a man can, like, be a fireman. Women can't lift a twenty-stone bloke on their shoulders, they've just got to accept it.* Otherwise it's not fair.

Reconstructed men generally find defensive men rather tiresome. The arguments are well worn, so when they are presented as brave and new, it can be very frustrating. Gerald Milligan, not surprisingly, had views on this subject:

> The backlash is so boring, it was bound to happen, I suppose. All I want to say to its proponents is, 'Hi guys, so, you've woken up to the fact that society is changing under your feet. Only took you twenty years, well done.' I don't normally like sarcasm, but it's difficult not to be a little sarcastic when it comes to the sad outpourings of these journalists. Women have only just started to get a little toe on the bottom rung of the ladder of power and already we have men foaming at the mouth. I cannot see what the fuss is about. I'm happy to look around the world, see what we men have done, after being in power for the last 3,000 years, shrug my shoulders, smile and say, 'Okay, we fucked up.'

* I claimed to be interested in this statement, and asked Bill to demonstrate how a man could lift a twenty-stone bloke on his shoulders. We asked his office colleague to assist us, a rather overweight gentleman by the name of Ted. Bill got Ted's feet off the ground for over a second. He's been seeing a back specialist ever since.

chapter 6
The Reconstructed Lifestyle

Dress Sense

Not many reconstructed men would be classified as 'fashionable' in the sense that they can be seen to be wearing the latest youth-oriented look. If they are over thirty, which at time of writing the vast majority in my study group are, they will all have matured gracefully in their dress codes.

They make a great effort not to make too great an effort when it comes to clothing, the relaxed, casual, 'I just threw something on before I came out' look is deemed essential. This takes hours and hours of careful choice, colour matching and accessorising before the reconstructed man hits the streets.

Matthew Carlton reveals all.

> The other day I had a lunch appointment with two business women. As an art director I am allowed to be a little eccentric in my dress, but knowing that they have to be fairly formal and are used to dealing with men in suits, I thought I'd dress down. I didn't want to

> embarrass them in public. I put on an open collar shirt, chunky knitwear pullover and loose-fitting American cut cotton trousers. I paraded in front of my live-in lover and the mirror. I decided it was too casual and put on my Tommy Nutter herringbone three-piece suit, a blue cotton button down collar shirt, colourful tie and a pair of black brogue shoes. This, I was sure was too formal, too 80s and too status-conscious, so out come the jeans, freshly washed and stiff as a board, and L.L. Bean shirt and casual baggy artists cut jacket. By this time my live-in lover was screaming at me to make up my mind. She was walking up and down our entrance lobby rattling the keys to her Golf.

This shows a greatly increased level of attention to dress amongst the average middle class reconstructed men.

There have always been men who preen and prune themselves, peacocks who go in for dramatic display. A sight which is only too common in London, Paris, Milan, Sydney, New York and Los Angeles in particular is a thirty-eight year old man, almost completely bald except for a pony tail, who is slightly too short and tubby to be wearing a two-tone Italian suit, fluorescent orange lycra turtle neck shirt with large gold pendant, and Air Jordan training shoes. He could be called a man who has his finger on the fluctuating tastes of his culture or he could be called a sad fuck fashion victim. The reconstructed man would never dress like this, not now. On the other hand he may end up dressing like it in ten years time, not when it has gone out of date, but when it is slightly more acceptable.

If there is any area that a reconstructed man is slightly conservative about, it's his dress sense. He knows this, and isn't threatened by it, he is dealing with this desire not to stand out too much on a daily basis.

One interesting dress code which I noticed was popular amongst a wide range of reconstructed men was the conventional shirt, top button done up, but no tie. I asked Gerald Milligan if he had any idea of the significance of this particular quirk.

> The shirt with no tie is a statement, there's no doubt about that. I think it says two things. One, I am not like other men who wear ties. I am flouting convention, but only enough to change your opinion by suggestion, not command. Two, and this is far more important, particularly in relation to women, the lack of tie says, I have a phallus, but it is hidden from view, therefore I am not sexually available to you at this time. I do not have to display my phallus as I have come to terms with it, but I am not a man without a phallus. My phallus is real and I have no need to show it. I think a lot of women don't realise this. For example, after working with a woman for three years, I never wore a tie in the office. When we finally went out on a date together, I wore a tie. I was showing her my phallus. It worked like a dream.

Cars

This is a contentious area becase most reconstructed men are keenly ideologically aware and consider cars and car culture in particular to reek of normal male values.

I asked Gerald Milligan if he drove a car, and if so, what sort.

> I do drive, very occasionally, when there is no other mode of transport. I have a Saab turbo, a black one, very sturdy car. I'm not at all interested in it, although I can see the aesthetic appeal, the way the wheel arches wrap around the impressively wide tyres. I don't really enjoy driving, but I decided that if I had to I may as well have a car that can push you back into your seat fairly effortlessly in all five gears. I have noticed some women are slightly impressed by my car. I always claim not to know anything about them when in this situation, although I did rebuild the gearbox one weekend. I don't like cars, except that new Renault mid-engine sports model. Beautiful, as an object, but it is fundamentally, a 150-mile-an-hour rocket. Not that I'm impressed, and I'd never buy one. I mean, who would buy a car that cost more than a house, when the money is enough to feed a small African country for a year and a half. It's a joke. But it does have a beautiful leather interior. It's a difficult area.

This sort of confusion is not shared by normal men, as can be seen on any busy major city route at any time of the day. Huge streams of traffic, and according to a recent survey in twelve cities nationally, 82% of private cars carry a single male occupant on 90% of journeys.

John Blake is one of those drivers. Due to his work, he spends a great deal of time behind the wheel of his beloved Ford Scorpio, thrashing up and down this small island's mass of congested highways.

> It's a big, thirsty, heavy motor. I love it. I sink back into the velour in the morning, press my foot hard down and feel that great two-point-eight-litre motor tear away at the road. It's a car that impresses the ladies, they know that the sort of man who drives it is basically in the

> executive area in life. A man who means business. I can see them casting an appreciative eye over my bodywork as I drive past. If I get the chance I'll try and make the tyres screech at traffic lights. I can tell that impresses women. They can see I'm the sort of man that appreciates good service, fine quality gift items and hard core pornography. The Ford Scorpio has a handy door pocket for that.

So, amongst the normal population, it would seem the car is still seen as a way men can identify themselves, which gives rise to many clichés still in current use. If people simply assume that a vehicle with a long bonnet means the male owner has a short stubby penis and is trying to make up for it, they are way off target.

With the advent of rear and mid-engined cars, and the wide range of GT fuel injected hatchbacks available,* the long bonnet is a thing of the past. Nonetheless, research† tells us a man who drives a 'sporty' car does so to try and counteract an underlying sexual problem.

It is a subject in which advertising agencies are obviously interested. If they are trying to sell a sporty GTi hatchback to a thirty-five-year-old man, and they discover that he is almost inevitably going to be hung like a gnat, they are going to use language and images which will re-assure him that, in this car, that will no longer be a problem.

They will use terms like 'nifty', 'small, but wiry' or 'the

* Not that I know anything about all this.

† Fiat, Ford and Renault all funded research by the Riewelt Foundation in Belgium to investigate the links between male sexual dysfunction, and the 0-60 times of various 'performance' cars. They discovered that, quite simply, the faster the car, the more the men felt that their phallic statistic was below average.

stubby one that packs a punch' to describe the vehicle, and therefore the driver. It is clear then that the advertising industry assumes that a car says a great deal about its owner, within our culture.

I wanted to know if reconstructed men thought a car defined who they were. I asked Matthew Carlton for his opinion.

> I hope not. I drive a Peugeot 205 GTi, it's full of junk. I'm just not interested in cars. I hate having one. I admit that quite often I will deny having one. I have a rack on the back of mine which holds a push bike. Quite often I'll drive to near a friend's house, park up and cycle the last half mile. I realise there's an element of hypocrisy there, but no more than I can deal with.

There seems to be a genuine reaction against cars. It may only be within the more radical elements at present, but it appears to be building. Nick Chisholm has a radical approach to the motor car.

> I have just sold my Audi Quattro, kept its value pretty well actually, not that I was interested. The thing is, and this fact has surprised a few of my friends, I'm not buying another. I live in the middle of a large city and I've said to myself, 'I do not need a car.' I've had to say it to myself daily over a three-year period as I have, like many Westerners, become totally dependent on having a vehicle. But now I am finally weaned. I use a push bike or public transport. If the bus is full, or running late, then I get a cab. I still wince a bit when people ask what sort of car I have and I say none, but I'm dealing with it.

Sport

I've quite often been asked what sort of sporting activity a reconstructed man would engage in, and my immediate response would be that most reconstructed men would find aggressive, competitive, contact sports fairly unattractive, as they smack of old-style, normal male values.

I have come across reconstructed footballers, rugby players and boxers, but they are few and far between. The most common sports with reconstructed participants seem to be athletics, swimming and cycling. Contact sports seem, in the main, to be more popular with normal or defensive men.

I asked Terry Sanderson, a man I classified as deeply defensive, if he thought the fact that he liked to play amateur soccer meant he was more sexist than right on reconstructed men.

> That's typical feminist nonsense. I like a game of soccer, it's healthy, get out there with your mates, spit, shout, swear and kick a ball about. It's not sexist. It's just a short time each week where we can get away from bickering women for a bit. What's wrong with that. It's not fair, women are always getting together and slagging off men. Why can't we do it? But oh no. It just proves we're all sexist lads. It's just not fair.

Gerald Milligan is very keen on athletics and weight training. He can be found on the track or in the gym for two or three hours each day.

> I wouldn't say I was obsessed, but when I passed thirty I suddenly understood that my life was finite, and that I'd better stay healthy. I am now ten times fitter than I was

at eighteen, I have a rock hard, ripped, chiselled torso, great flexibility, that's from yoga; amazing stamina, that's jogging, sprinting, cycling and swimming; strength from weight training and good skin from a wide range of facial products. I know I am far more attractive to women, being in super tip-top physical shape. Ironically, exercising at the level I do plays havoc with my sexual drives. I don't have any, I have no energy for sex. I don't fall asleep after making love, I usually nod off just before. This is quite annoying for women, and I can see why.

Money

This was a very interesting area to ask reconstructed men about. I got the feeling that although a lot of them had done an enormous amount of work on the private, sexual and domestic areas of their lives, their attitudes to money were somewhat confused.

As I stated earlier, the men I talked to come from a wide range of economic backgrounds, but if I was less generous (or more honest), I would have to say that most of the reconstructed men I spoke to were, to use an unpleasant 80s phrase, 'pulling down a comfortable amount of K per annum'.

It's a truth that has to be faced that men who can afford the time and energy to spend navel gazing for a few years on the road to reconstruction will have to be financially 'well hung'. They are acutely aware of this, and will often introduce each new notion or opinion with a phrase along the lines of, '*of course, I realise I'm very lucky in being able to afford the time to spend three weeks in a sweat lodge*'.

Matthew Carlton has no illusions about the role money had to play in his journey to reconstruction.

> My first weekend intensive course cost me three hundred and eighty pounds. That was ten years ago. I heard recently about a genital balancing weekend in Scotland which cost a thousand pounds a head for two days. Okay, so I know not a lot of men can afford to spend that sort of money, but in some ways it's a question of priorities. I didn't spend it on beer, cigarettes or prostitutes, but then I have to say that I could afford beer, cigarettes, prostitutes *and* genital balancing weekend intensives. Not that I do of course.

Donald Wallace, the architect, has less problem dealing with money. He told me in a good year he makes as much as £150,000. He hasn't had a good year for a while, but he's surviving. His attitude to money is very philosophical.

> I used to refer to money as 'green energy' when I was a hippy architect student. We all looked upon money as a very negative thing in those days, something that sapped your creative strength. That attitude came out of a watered-down appraisal of Marxist economics which has been somewhat undermined in recent years. I now feel that when I'm offered truly large sums of money, my creative juices flow. I find money erotic, I'm not ashamed to say it. I'll say it now. The sight of a very large cheque, and I'm talking six to eight figures here, well, to be frank it can make me hard.

Reconstructed men are in many ways more adept at dealing with the guilt and shame that large salaries can induce amongst the liberal middle class in Britain. In the seventies, for example, a humanities lecturer who was earning a respectable wage would be crippled with guilt, would drive a battered Citroen covered in CND and Save the Whale stickers, and would have homeless foreign students living in his house.

The normal man of the same period would have no trouble earning a large income, and would want to make sure everyone knew about it. Harry Fleming told me about when he first started to earn big money.

> I admit I did spend a lot at first, mainly on gold ornaments for the house. I wanted to 'feel' rich, so, you know, I had a lot of gold jewellery, heavy stuff, a Cartier watch, gold identity bracelet etc. We had gold taps fitted, I even got a gold toothbrush. That was classic, it wasn't an antique, well, you wouldn't want to stuff some dead bloke's toothbrush in your mouth. It was based on a Roman design, like a gold Roman toothbrush. My wife said I was neuvo rich or something, so I bought her a new Burgundy all leather suite and she shut up.

More recently many reconstructed men have made positive steps away from the struggle for wealth. They are all 100% behind getting some other sort of fulfilment out of their work. Nick Chisholm, who we met earlier, would be very prepared to live on less money if he enjoyed his work.

> I've always loathed the notion of working just for the money, being a wage slave. If I don't find fulfilment from my work, then I stop doing it. I am not the slightest bit interested in what I get paid. I know that I am very lucky, working in television, because I am totally fulfilled by what I do and I earn a huge amount of

money. I don't know how much and I don't want to find out, but I never seem to run out.

Health

The male attitude to health, outside the world of health professionals, has very often been a taboo area. Because part of the essence of 'being a man' has been the open manifestation of virile physical strength and the ability to endure hardship, discussion of physical ailments has often been seen as a weakness. Geoff Pickering, a normal man from Surrey who we've met before, had a lot to say on this subject. He has a history of poor health.

> Other chaps don't want to know if you're poorly. I never told anyone about my sickness. It wouldn't be right, and anyway, a sick elephant is left behind by the herd. A chap at my office just upped and died one day, heart probably. All the ladies rallied around, but the men just carried on working. We didn't want to know you see. Different attitude to the whole thing. Maybe it comes from the war. I don't know. I wasn't in it myself, did my National Service peeling potatoes in Cyprus.

Nowadays, due to a more 'holistic' approach to the body, the environment and health, people, and men in particular, are far more aware of the day-to-day functions of their bodies. Some might see this as obsessive or hypochondriac behaviour, but many doctors I've spoken to have admitted that having patients who are more conversant with the workings of their bodies is generally to be encouraged, although one or two confessed to me privately that having someone who'd read a lot of books about health could prove to be a complete pain in the ass.

Gerald Milligan is a forerunner of a reconstructed attitude to personal health.

> My health is of vital importance to me. I think it's safe to say I have not had a day's illness for the past four years. I have kept detailed computerised daily recordings of my temperature, blood pressure, heart rate and sperm count for the last two years. It makes fascinating reading and I quite often print it out for friends. It's also very useful when consulting your doctor, even though mine begs me not to bring in too much data.

We can see a huge change in attitudes here. No longer is the health of the male a dark guarded secret. You will always know you have met a reconstructed man if he shows you the scars from an operation, tells you how to check for testicular cancer or reinforces the importance of foreskin hygiene in uncircumcised men as a way to avoid penile cancer.

He will know which vitamins you need to avoid early hair loss, libido loss, tooth loss or sight and hearing loss. He will know the best accupuncturist, herbalist, healer, colour therapist and osteopath in the local area. He will suggest the best mouthwash, eye wash, facial scrub and hair shampoo. He will have tips on shaving, hair care, ear wax and smegma problems. He will always know a lot of people who are fatally ill, have just died, or who will probably die if they don't stop what they are doing.

Normal men, it goes without saying, usually become horrifically aware that fifty-eight years of executive-style lunches and sitting in the Cavalier SRi are bad for them as they clutch their chests and collapse in hotel foyers.

Self-loathing men have a slightly different attitude to health problems, as Frank Jessop explains.

> I had a rash under my arm once, typical, it was my own fault for not drying properly after I had a bath. I don't like bathing, I think it's a waste of water, but then I smell and that's so typically male. Sometimes I sit in the bathroom and cry, trying to work out what to do. Male self-pity, typical. I went to my doctor with the rash, but because she's a woman, I was sure she had better things to do, like treating rape victims and battered wives, so I left. The rash got worse, went gangrenous and I had to have my arm amputated. Typical blocked male attitude to illness. I make myself sick. No wonder no one visited me in hospital. I don't blame them.

Restaurants

A weakness I discovered amongst the vast majority of reconstructed men I met – who otherwise were very modest in their tastes, humble in their desires and super aware of any elitist activity – was good quality restaurants. This surprised me as they all claimed to be good cooks, and often were, but if ever I suggested conducting an interview in a restaurant, a reconstructed man would always become more interested in what I was trying to do.

There doesn't seem to be any specific type of 'reconstructed restaurant', though the trendy, pseudo-French wine bar type places with poor quality French style food items did not score very highly.

Thai food, Italian, Indian and good quality French seemed to be the most popular – busy restaurants with a continental flavour, which reminded them of periods they've spent overseas. Donald Wallace had this to say as we were eating in ZenW3, a reconstructed Chinese restaurant in Hampstead, North London.

> I love this place because they don't use any monosodium glutamate, and there's a constant flow of exciting young people coming in and out. I don't really approve of eating out on moral grounds, but that is the puritanical protestant side of me, which I understand but like to keep under control. The continental Catholic, debauched and social side loves eating out. The hubub, the comings and goings, the eyes flashing across the room, it makes eating an exciting event. It's very sexual here, eating and sex, they walk arm in arm, let's face it. I love both, being a sensualist.

Holidays

Again, it was hard to get a picture of a typical reconstructed holiday. I heard opinions as widely different as Matthew Carlton's:

> I go on holiday in mass-transit Spanish-beach-front package holiday type places, to avoid the horrible elitist, 'got to get away from it all' type experience. I love people, all types, I love mixing with them. I have a great time, I love working class women as they are much more honest. If I approach one for sex, it's a yes or no response. I have a great time. It's very refreshing.

right through to Peter Harris:

> I never go on holiday. The way I see it, and I don't want to be too critical of people who do, but if your life is so miserable all year round, and you have to go away for two weeks to make it bearable, change your life. Stop what you are doing and make your life interesting, beautiful, useful and fulfilling. Then we wouldn't waste our time and destroy other people's countries by having to 'be on holiday'.

Domestic Taste

This is an area which has seen a large and ever-increasing gender shift in the past few years. Only ten or twenty years ago, you could walk into a furniture or interior decor shop and you would see couples walking around choosing their home furnishings, fabrics and fittings. The woman would be bug-eyed with interest and excitement, the man would be barely awake. He would have spent the previous five days slogging his guts out in the workplace; the last thing he wanted to do was traipse around a stuffy furniture shop and be fauned on by obsequious staff.

Today that picture is changing. I spent two afternoons behind the counter in a large central London furniture store. I watched the people coming and going and made copious notes. The first big change I noticed was the number of men who were making what is known in the retail trade as 'purchase decisions'. Again and again I heard the men saying, '*Well, you like it don't you?*' while the women nodded and looked tired.

The structure of that sentence was vital. It wasn't '*Do you like it?*', asking for reassurance, not feeling confident about the purchase. It was exactly the opposite, a question only out of politeness. '*You like it don't you?*' meaning, '*if you don't, you can stuff your opinion because this is what we're having.*'

As we have seen earlier, this is merely a manifestation of the power shift between men and woman, but leading experts in the field see a shift taking place in our interior design tastes.

Wallace Hooper, one of the top interior designers in New York, has noticed a big increase in male tastes over the last few years. He said:

> Only a few years ago it was chintz, chintz, chintz. Everything was patterned and had a frilly border. Lots of floral, lots of tassels, lots of bright, bright colours. Occasionally I would do a study and go for the dark oak, whiskey and open fire, leather-bound, Ralph Lauren polo pony look. Now it's all cream walls, colourless, plain quality fabrics, light distressed oak, lovely shades of blue and white in cushions. It's not hard masculinity, it's more a freshly shaven chin in a Pacific breeze. Very clean, strong, with beautiful lines. I'd say we were looking at butch in the 21st century.

chapter 7

Sex

The Role of Human Feelings in Feeling Humans

Sex is an inevitable subject when writing about the relations between people. Sex absorbs a huge part of our waking consciousness, directs and drives our cultures and keeps us on the planet. It is seen by some as the great leveller, the thing we all want, nearly all of us have, and we only start to tire talking about in our late sixties.*

So much has been written about sex, so many books, pamphlets and kinky playing cards have been produced that it's clear it is a popular subject. That said, this book is an attempt to break down many of those expectations, to throw the cliché up into the air and blow it out of the sky with the pump-action shotgun of integrity.†

Therefore there is no information about reconstructed attitudes to foreplay, nipple-tickling, fellatio, non-genital-

* I have come across plenty of examples of people well past retirement age who tell me of goings on in pre-war suburbia which made Madonna and Julian Clary look like outrageous sexually open individuals.

† I will grant that this is a rather macho piece of terminology, but I think it describes the strength of feeling behind the statement.

focused stimulation with feathers,* cunnilingus, rimming, condoms, penetration, copulation or general safe sex practices. There will be no lurid descriptions of a safe-sex video produced in America, containing vivid and brightly-lit scenes of how it's done, done well, done kinky and done safe.†

I shall, because I am writing about heterosexuality, naturally be dealing with heterosexual relations. This could be seen as ignoring the fact that there are plenty of reconstructed gay men around. In fact, as a general rule, gay men set the pace in male awareness of sexual politics. They have always been far more in touch with their feelings, and many straight men owe a huge debt of gratitude to gay men who have helped them crawl slowly towards some crude form of self-awareness.‡

This chapter is also written in full awareness of the fact that there are plenty of people to whom sex never has been a problem, it has merely been a source of great comfort and pleasure. When I meet people like that I have to deal with a desire to punch them, which I know is a very immature and unreconstructed response. This chapter then, is for the rest of us.

New Complications

One thing women could rely on in the past was a basic understanding of men and their sexual needs which would

* N.G.F.S.W.F.

† To quote the cover of the video box.

‡ Some readers may notice an element of autobiography creeping into this statement. If they did, I have to take my hat off to their perceptive abilities.

stand them in good stead for their whole life. Normal men are simple. They may be arrogant and aggressive, even violent and dangerous, but they are essentially seen by women as being simple to understand. Their lusts and needs were understood by every woman; any attempt made by men to display their feelings elicited a gentle understanding smile, such as a mother would give watching her baby take her first steps.

The reconstructed man, as we have already seen, tends to challenge a lot of the stereotypical behaviour women have come to expect. This challenge isn't intended as an aggressive display, throwing down the gauntlet in a dominant patriarchal stance to maintain the *status quo*. It's intended as a gentle move to alter the way men and women relate to each other across the gender divide. It has come about through a greater understanding of themselves as men.

This greater understanding brings with it a far greater complexity in dealings between the genders. All our assumptions are shattered, all our preconceived notions of how we should behave and respond are thrown to the winds. The reconstructed man will always go the way the woman least expects, always have the argument to hand that the woman has never dreamed of, the excuse that sounds most plausible.

No reconstructed man will ever assume a woman wants to have sex simply because he does. This is not because he is lazy, study group member Peter Bradshaw, a twenty-seven-year-old musician explains:

> Historically, she's been put under immense pressure to be sexually available to me. I don't want to burden women with this role, or myself with the guilt that

> accompanies my advances. I therefore use the theory that eventually any woman will become sexually needy if I wait in her bed long enough.

If a woman finds this reticence a problem, there is an easy solution. She merely needs to describe his behaviour as passionless. For a reconstructed man to be defined as passionless is as bad as calling a normal man penis-less. Reconstructed men are very interested in passion, they will haved studied it in depth over a long period. Doug McGuinness, a thirty-three-year-old industrial design lecturer, is revealing on this subject.

> When she told me she thought I was passionless, I had to sit in silence and think about it for a week. People thought I was sulking, but I was working it out. I went out and bought books about passion and decided to give it a go. I went round to her house and threw myself at her feet. I sobbed and threatened to disembowel myself there and then because I loved her so much. She said she didn't believe me, she said it looked like I'd read a book about passion and was trying it out. I tried not to be threatened by her insights. I then started working on passionate facial and arm gesticulation exercises with an Italian therapist.

Once you've got through the initial courting period and discover he's not a very good sexual partner, at least he'll be able to talk about it. Things have slowly improved; through representations in the media and late-night discussion programmes on television, the British male lover has slowly hauled himself unwillingly from beneath the sweaty eiderdown of his forebears and revealed himself in his true light to the world.

The response has not been encouraging, some women have been disparaging and cruel, but this is only to be expected when you take our mutual histories into consideration.

This said, a woman should find that a reconstructed man is a slightly better bet between the sheets. The whole presentation of the male body 'package' will be under-played and neat; no showy boxer shorts with clown noses here – either a designer jock strap in grey or black, or instant nudity with no hang-ups. Resonant flatulence in bed will not, as has historically always been the case, be regarded as a source of long-term humour. This is not to say a reconstructed man will not laugh. But as Gerald Milligan says, 'I'd only laugh to help cover my lover's embarrassment and distaste.'

He will be open and loving in his sexual actions, but unlike the idealised photographs of perfect couples that adorn the pages of our glossy leisure magazines, he may be a little more complex. Doug Philips explains:

> There's no need for a woman to talk dirty in order to sexually arose me. On the other hand if she felt like experimenting with mirrors, cameras, rubber, leather or low-impact sadomasochism, I would be a willing and helpful partner. In order not to feel repressed I will of course need to talk about these activities a great deal with her friends, her family, especially her father.

chapter 8

Why Bother?

I am often asked by men if I really believe that attempting to change male behaviour and outlook is worth all the bother. It can be quite surprising where this question will come up. For example I'll be in the supermarket, enjoying doing my share of the housework, choosing new food products and comparing prices. I'll notice a man in a suit standing holding a trolley while his partner chooses what to eat. He will be bored and listless, no doubt having sexual fantasies about a famous TV actress taking her clothes off and lying naked on a four-poster bed. He will then spot me and it all seems too much for him. He'll come up to me and pin me by the throat to the canned fruit section, an area I'm unfamiliar with as I only buy fresh fruit. He'll ask me, between clenched teeth, if I really think all this rubbish about men changing their behaviour is going to do anyone any good in the long run.

When he finally lets me go, I suggest we talk about it quietly in my consulting rooms and give him my card. However, the question is an interesting one. Society is changing slowly, but it is changing. Even the most normal of men have begun to notice there are more women at work; there are even, very occasionally, women who are in a position of power over them, a particularly galling experience for a normal man.

Some intellectuals might argue that the difference between a reconstructed and unreconstructed man is impossible to measure. It's certainly very subtle in places. There are plenty of men who not only see any attempt at change as a complete waste of time, some defensive men don't even believe it's possible. One of my interviewees, Richard Mallace said:

> Men just get better at lying. All this talk about looking after babies and doing the washing up. We don't want to do that, why pretend. It's a load of wank isn't it. Women don't want us fussing round the house, we should be out doing male things. It's much simpler that way. Anyway, women are so thick, my wife doesn't know diddley squit, she's dumb, she can't deal with the daily grind of decision making like I have to. I have to live with the fact that I'm a bloody wage slave until I die at fifty-eight and my wife lives off my pension. She only has to be a housewife, a whore and a baby machine as bloody middle class snot nosed feminists would have it. You can legislate all you like, it's not going to change biology is it. Hey, is that tape recorder on? You said this was off the record. What's my wife going to think? You know-all bastard.*

This was such a negative response that I combed through all my research looking for something to counter-balance it. It took me a long time. Reconstructed men are nothing

* Richard and I have had a long and complex professional relationship. He is fundamentally a good person I think. Certainly people who come into brief contact with him would find him highly abrasive, defensive and obviously deeply insecure. He uses verbal aggression to keep people at a safe distance. I showed his wife this quote and the rest of the interview and she left him that day. He has of course, decided to focus the blame for the break-up of his family on myself, which is an entirely predictable example of blame re-alignment.

if not realistic, they are sceptical about the whole process. The mood in sexual politics in recent years has certainly been one of retrenchment. Many of the gains of early feminist struggle have been worn away by recession, reaction and the re-emergence of patriarchal pride, built on bullshit as personified by bitter defensive men.

The Influence of Reconstructed Men on Society

It would seem from my exhaustive research that reconstructed men are the only non-negative reaction to feminism. They may not be perfect, right or even very interesting, but everything else is pretty awful in comparison. What conclusion can we come to when we look at this odd, indeed very rare, breed of men? We shouldn't for a moment put them on a pedestal and admire them. They are, like everyone, a product of their environment. Maybe we should however, look at them every now and then to see what they're doing. For one thing, to put the whole debate in perspective, it's worth looking at whether reconstructed men have had any effect on society at large.

As we can see by this representation, many of the concepts I've been discussing have yet to make a large impact on the world. In fact the statistics used to create this image come from the London School of Optimistic Studies, which tries to find positive results in seemingly negative socio-economic forecasts from around the word. With the best will in the world they could only muster a

0.00042% reading on the number of men who care about, or are even interested in, the whole gamut of questions brought up in the subject-area of sexual politics and the relationships between the genders.

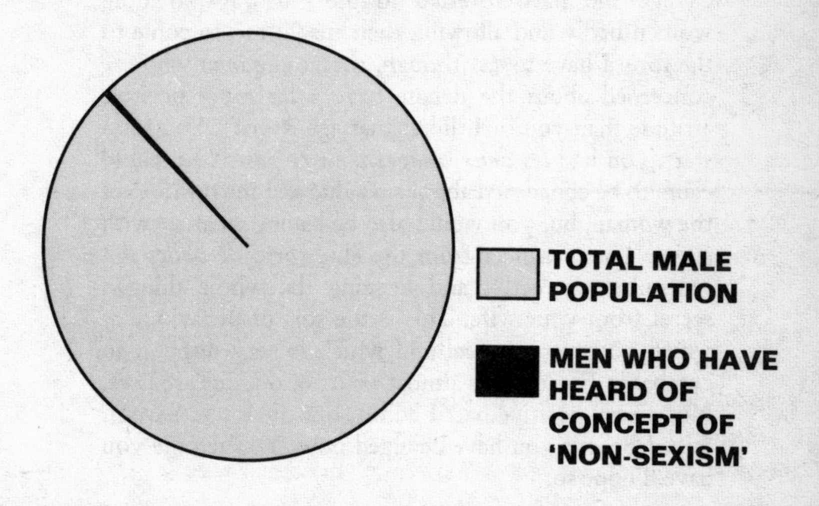

I decided to try to find some of the other academics who *are* interested, in the hope that their opinions might shine some light and offer a glimmer of hope.

I started with an old associate, Professor Christian Vergule of the Paris-based, Institute De Sexualité Humaine. He has been working both on himself as an individual and on his students as a group since the mid 1960s. I wanted to ask if he had noticed any change and if he was prepared to state that it was a change for the better. He said:

> As you know the position is slightly different in my country. We don't have to deal with the same level of paranoid misogyny as you do in Britain, but we are still living in a post patriarchal period of deep chaos and psycho-sexual disorder. Many of my younger students have shunned the efforts of their older brothers to change and have reverted to the old ways, treating women badly and allowing their machismo to come to the fore. I have to say though, the young men who *are* concerned about the debate have a far more positive attitude than you or I did at that age Robert. You for a start, you had *les deux visages n'est ce pas?* You would claim to be concerned about sexualité and the position of the woman, but you would also be having an affair with a very young dancer from the élite *corps de ballet* if I remember correctly, and keeping the whole thing a secret from your wife. This is the sort of behaviour of which you were critical and which is very difficult to combat in France. It is almost a part of our culture here. Not a very positive part I admit, but there you have it. Still, I believe you have changed now. You tell me you have. I hope so.*

Christian works within French academic circles and is therefore bound to have a slightly different view. I decided to ask someone who at least works within the same language as Britain, so I talked to someone whose work I had admired for many years, John D. Speffendaffer, author of the American bestseller, *Men Who Like Women For*

* I have to say that Christian has a very one-sided view of what was, on reflection, a very sophisticated but admittedly sex-based relationship I had with a dancer called Yasmine Carbouche. True, she was only 18, but I was a mere thirty-six at the time, hardly old enough to be her father. Anyway, it's all sorted out now. Meaning I got away with it.

About Ten Minutes Then Get All Iffy and Run Off Without Explanation,* what he thought about the influence of the reconstructed man. He said:

> Their influence is going to appear large but in effect be very small. Many of the men you have defined as reconstructed are now in positions of power. They could effect social planning in hyper-beneficial ways if they operate correctly. Most of them are very concerned about the role of women in society, they are challenging the stereotypes, banning pornography from the work-place and organising mass men's days within their own office environments. Men who aren't prepared to change are going to be left out of the breeding cycle like wounded ducks. The modern American woman just doesn't have time to 'sort out' her partner. She has her own career commitments to deal with; if he can't handle child care planning, there's going to be no amazing American sex sessions. The next few years are either going to be fascinating or boring. It's impossible to say which. But hey Bob, basically, at the end of the day, guys like to ball, and chicks like security, so you've got a basic conflict which keeps people like us in a job, don't knock it man.

So, what conclusion can we draw? Is there any point in men trying to change themselves? Has all the soul-searching, pontificating and publishing in the last twenty years been in vain? There are certainly many elements within our society who would hope so. This is not to imply

* John Speffendaffer wrote this book in the mid 1980s and readily admits that it is now out of date. Since then he has written the American bestseller, *Women Who Love Men Who Had a Difficult Time Relating To Their Fathers And Wish They Could Change And See A Woman As A Way To Their Own Personal Salvation But Tend to Wear Her Out With Their Emotional Demands*, published by Tossario books, New York and Boston.

that all those elements would be men. There are many retrograde and reactionary women who want 'men to be men', whatever that is supposed to mean.

Have Things Changed Over the Last Twenty Years?

I am dealing here, however, with the male of the species, so to sum up the last twenty years I include interviews with each of the four types of men I've defined – normal, defensive, self-loathing and reconstructed.

One of the more remarkable, and for my money most enjoyable normal men I interviewed, John Blake, the biochemist from Chelmsford, was quite forthcoming when I asked him if he thought men had changed at all over the last twenty years. He said:

> Look, ladies are ladies, and blokes are blokes, no one wants to change. It was all fine until you lot of God botherers and do gooders messed it all up. It's so confusing now, I don't know where I stand any more. Tell a joke in a pub and you get your head bitten off. I get dizzy with all the different stuff going on. And how come you're so sorted out, eh? How come all the ladies like you, what the hell do they see in you, that's what I want to know, smug git.

It is clear that John Blake sees a post-patriarchal society as a dark, dangerous and confusing place. This notion fits very neatly with many post Freudian theories of male sexual fear. John Blake fears chaos, the chaos which surrounds him now that women have started answering back. What he really fears is the chaos he knows is inside him. He fears the explosion which might result if, for a moment, he 'let go'. This is all primary psycho-sexual material and not too much should be read into it. John Blake needs to be encouraged to let go within a secure padded environment with a fully qualified professional at his side armed to the teeth with heavy suppressant drugs, preferably in dart-gun format.

Simon Young, the first defensive man I quoted was furious when I suggested that men might not have changed that much in the last twenty years. He said:

> Of course we've changed, we've been forced to by the fascism of feminism. The 'no' generation, no you can't say cunt, no you can't tell rape jokes, no we won't suck your cocks, no no no. That's all we get from women, we try to help out, I've done the drying-up. But it's gone too far, if women ruled the world we'd be at war every month. We have to put up with their bloody hormones, they outlive us and spend all our money when we're dead, they set our children against us. I tell you, the one thing I want to change at the moment is the clock. Turn the fucking thing back to 1890, children should be seen and not heard, women lie back and think of England. Look how powerful and respected we were then. It's not fair, women have spoilt it all.

The antidote to that attitude, and the next step that many men have to go through, is the self-loathing man. Timothy Whetstone personifies this state of mind for me. Tall, well built, bit of a beer gut, kind face, utterly downtrodden by bitter short-haired women with enough of their own problems to last a lifetime. But Timothy sees it as all his fault. The last twenty years have been hard for him.

> I don't think men have changed over the last twenty years, we've just got worse. More dirty, more loathsome, I mean, my cock has got more ugly as I've grown older. It now looks like a small unwrapped pack of turkey giblets. It's revolting. Why should any woman allow me to rub that against her, all proddy and pokey. I'm disgusting, no one knows just how bad, but I'm bad inside, believe me. Worse than you think.

Finally, Peter Bradshaw, a founder member of my study group, has been on his personal journey, stumbling and crawling toward reconstruction over the last twenty years. I asked him for his opinion on changing male attitudes and how he felt he had changed since the start of my study period way back in the heady days of the early seventies. He said:

> In the seventies I tried to be open. In the eighties I tried to be honest. In the nineties I'm going to kick some ass. That was what I said to my analyst on New Year's Eve 1990. I was drunk. I'm dealing with the embarrassment connected with that statement now, in a non-threatened, adult and mature way.

On reflection, Peter is not really a very good example of what constitutes a reconstructed man. The study of male responses to feminism is to say the least, not an exact science.

However, one phenomenon which has emerged is male emotional literacy. The ability to describe the emotional nuances of one's journey. Study group member Gerald Milligan is a master of this, and so I decided to leave the last word to him – a final reminder of the pitfalls of such an arduous journey towards enlightenment.

Gerald Milligan:

> I used to think honesty was paramount, now I'm not so sure. I think being sensitive is more important. By sensitive I mean understanding other people's feelings and blending your truth to suit them. It's not lying exactly, it's the adaptation of reality. In a way allowing people to believe what they want to believe about you.

Why Did I Bother?

One last thing, a question I am faced with time and time again. And it's totally understandable. People have often asked me: is this book and the very profitable lecture series derived from it really one of the most complex and involved ways of trying to pick up women ever attempted? Are all the theories really to do with trying to please a woman and re-assure her that I am not only fully and deeply reconstructed but also a great lover?

The question I get asked is, to put it succinctly, '*Did you write this book in order to get off with feminist women at lectures, book signings and seminars?*'

I hope the answer is burning off the page as you read this, I hope you can see the answer, hear it in fact, yelling at you. I feel it is almost an offence to write it down here, to jump to the assumption that you cannot tell for yourself. It is so painfully obvious that I am not going to soil the whole experience by writing it. You know.

The accusations that my work is only a complex and disturbing 'chat up' method come mostly from defensive men who are deeply threatened by what I have to say. Even if it were such an exercise, I have now reached a state of emotional maturity where the pointlessness and hollowness of a short-term, supposedly simple sexual experience is far, far outweighed by the more complex, confusing, irritating, ever-growing, fascinating experience I have with my long-term partner.

This is not to say that I don't find a lot of the women I meet through my work, deeply, deeply attractive. I do. I am only heterosexual.* Just because I deal with human sexuality and relationships on a professional level doesn't mean I have eliminated my own personal urges. Far from it. Constant temptation, however, is part of the journey towards a world of trust and long-term companionship.

* I have to admit that no one can state categorically what they will be doing in a week, a month or a year. I may very well still be involved in a very committed relationship involving children and other life-changing experiences. Alternatively I may not, and it is because of this possibility, and only because of this, that I have decided to release my mobile phone number. It is 0800 8332 199190.

Research Notes

All the surveys referred to in the book were conducted using standard pop psychology techniques as laid down by John D. Speffendaffer and Mary Tolleringham in their book, *How To Find Out What People Want To Read About Themselves*, which gave me many valuable insights. My research period covered a ten-year period between March 1979 and December 1989. Any information about the previous ten years, i.e. 1969-79, I have discovered by questioning people who were involved in the various movements mentioned. I spent time with men in prison in 1982, with men in a Melbourne men's house in 1990, with men around a campfire sweating and drumming in British Columbia in 1987. I lay in Los Angeles re-birth tanks in 1985, I cried in Lake District meditation centres in 1989. These were all vitally important moments in my journey towards the completion of this book. However, the vast majority of my really important research took place during the following events:

10 March 1979
In a warehouse next to the river Thames, a birthday party which degenerated into a political slanging match, the consensus being that the Labour party would get in at the next election because English men were too 'sexist' to vote for a woman as Prime Minister. Many of the women present that night claimed that Margaret Thatcher couldn't

be a woman really, because no woman could be that right wing. It's very easy to look back to those times now with the benefit of hindsight and laugh at people's stupidity. I love doing that.

16 May 1981
At a dinner party at Thelma Donaldson's house in Highgate. We had a lovely meal and talked about sex and men for about three hours. One of the men present got very drunk and told us we were all middle-class wankers and stormed out. We then discussed the concept of blame re-alignment before coffee and liqueurs and retiring to separate beds.

7 February 1983
I held a dinner party in a small flat in Islington with five people present. We discussed numerous topics regarding sexism and the women's movement, the treatment of women in the Third World and the international build up of guilt. I asked everyone present what they thought about various subjects and have used this survey to prove numerous theories. I tried to make a fruit pie but the pastry went very wrong and was the cause of much mirth. I decided to concentrate on cooking and other domestic chores and wrote numerous papers on the subject.

30 March 1984
At a dinner party in Rue Dauphine, Paris, in Jacques et François' astonishing roof-top apartment. I started the ball rolling by suggesting that I found French men less sexist. It was great, a virtual riot, one or two of the men tried to agree with me, but it was soon proved to me my theory was unjustified. We then spent five hours discussing the way women were portrayed in films, TV and French

pornography (which would cause a fire if hidden under the average English mattress). The arguments became very heated. I left at three-thirty and walked home with a friend.*

12 June 1985
A glorious night, Bar-B-Que in a back garden of Gerald Milligan's 'done up' house in Hackney. Present were a cocktail of liberal intellectuals, new men, feminists, gay activists and journalists which made this one of the best surveys I have ever conducted. I got involved in a row about child care provision and the systematic way women were being forced back into the home. By this time I was well dug into my kitchen and didn't want a woman butting her nose in. I developed theories during this event which have held in good shape for years.

16 August 1987
A large gathering at the house of good friend John D. Speffendaffer on La Cienega Boulevard, Los Angeles. The party mainly consisting of pundits, critics, writers, journalists, actors and minor television producers. In other words a healthy cross-section of American society. The interesting penomenon here was as the evening progressed, the men stayed around the buffet discussing their children's eduction and sexuality, while the women were standing near the drink exchanging some of the foulest jokes in the crudest language I have ever had the opportunity to eavesdrop on. After this evening I decided the whole of American sexual politics was reversed and the concept of sexism no longer existed there.

* No, it wasn't the 'young dancer' mentioned by Christian Vergule.

20 December 1988
A Christmas Party at the office of a left-wing graphic design collective in Bermondsey. Although a great deal of heavy drinking took place, a survey was conducted using this broad cross-section of people. Within this heady mix, professions ranged from teacher right through to lecturer, from graphic design consultant to people working in the field of experimentation with image and text. I fulfilled many long-term desires as regards surveys and managed to build up a dossier of social trends and emotional, society wide, meta-language.

17 July 1989
North Carlton, Melbourne. In the refurbished house of journalist Pete McBrachen, the beer flowed, the food was great, the women were very, very loud and drunk. Mostly lesbians, though there were three heterosexual women present. The men cooked and talked about cars and sport quietly in the corner. The women held sway, shouting over each other and bursting into screaming fits of laughter. The men seemed to have a great time, enjoying the ribald humour and the foul language. The women were very competitive and aggressive, the men softer and supportive; there was much hugging and back touching in the male camp. I naturally devised major, major reasons for this apparent role reversal.

New Year's Eve, 1989-90
A quiet event in the spacious kitchen of business women Siønead Maxwell and her partner, Guibert Daboulé. Here we talked Euro-sexuality until well after three, we compared notes on various nationalities, on sexual attitudes and assumptions in the USA and the third world.

We didn't come to any firm conclusions, but the hazy ideas that emerged as the night wore on have since become hardened theories which will take some considerable dislodging.

Bibliography

These are books which inspired and encouraged me in my work, but which I have made no direct reference to in the text.

What on Earth are Ladies Going on About? by Rev. Christopher Dickins, published by Truth Books, Basingstoke, 1989. Many valuable insights here from the confused Christian male. The Reverend Dickins is not overly keen on the ordination of women, seeing it as opening the flood gates of chaos and the arrival of the cloven hoofed one. Dreadful cover design typical of Truth Books, the publishing arm of the World Truth Corp, a nightmarish right-wing Christian pressure group from America.

Gender and Misery by Frances Gervais Milson published by The North London Free Trades Wholefood Co-op. Written in 1972, this book is so depressing it has to be read to be believed. It gave me very many useful ideas on guilt and suffering among the affluent well educated classes. The section on why women wear long dresses and chain smoke is a wonderful evocation of the period.

Men Are Wonderful by Barbara Cartland. Hard to get hold of this one, but a collectors' item. One of the best comedy books ever written by a woman whose insights and opinions never cease to astound. It is actually quite a short book, and very small.

Does Size Really Matter? by Philip Morrow and Peter Ward. Published by 21 Books, 1990. Morrow and Ward get them out and measure them, metaphorically of course, in this serious and depressing study of the male member.

Western Sexuality by Philippe Ariès and André Béjin, published by Blackwell. This one's a scream, two dour French intellectuals coming up with juicy facts about how our foremothers and -fathers used to do it. You think we're kinky and obsessed with sex in the 90s. We don't come close to the average fourteenth-century burger in his green tights, let me tell you.

Women Who Love So Much Their Men Feel A Bit Overwhelmed And Plead for Less Intimacy by Celia Catzenbreath, published by Decker and Talberg, New York, 1988. The title says it all really. Ms Catzenbreath comes to the conclusion that women are too emotional and should go to workshops to learn to block their emotions, repress their feelings and stifle any expression of love. This she believes is the only way career women are going to get a man. Typical of the rash of recent backlash books.

Iron John by Robert Bly, published by Element Books, 1991. The bible from the wild man of the mountain. Actually quite a nice book about ancient poetry and storytelling, and nothing to do with humping trees in the woods. Still, it's amazing what a bit of hype can do.

Drums, Fur, The Scream and The Sweat Lodge. Memoirs of

ten years of men's workshops by Frank Jissop published by Tulip books, 1990. Brilliant book this, some screamingly funny moments recorded of men taking themselves very seriously in the woods. If only a few normal men would do Mr Jissop's classes, but I can't seen them forking out four hundred odd quid to do so.

Male Fantasies I & II by Claus Theweliet. Published by Polity Press, 1986 and 1990. Titled in the original German *Männerphantasien*, these books chart the inner lives of the men of the Freikorps, the precursor to the Waffen SS and the Third Reich. Brilliant work by Theweliet; chilling, insightful and a stark reminder that any man is only a step away from that Uniform and those Boots. For me the message was, watch out guys, there but for a different dress code and surrounding political environment go the lot of us. Another reason I like these books is the covers look great on my book shelves.